CHOCOLATE SAUCE

THE PLAIN VANILLA ASTROLOGER'S GUIDE TO THE ART OF PRACTICING ASTROLOGY

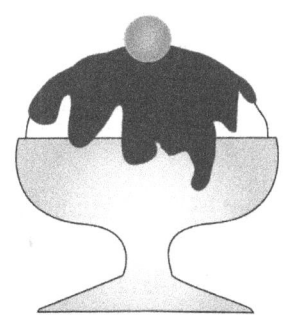

Pat Geisler

ACS Publications

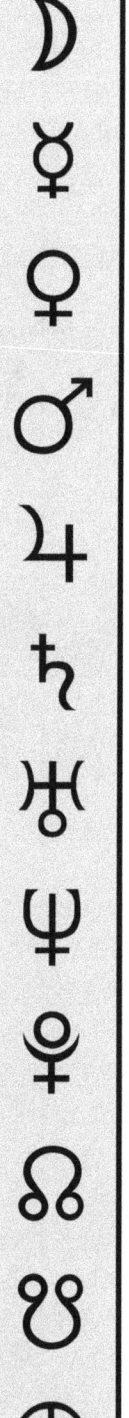

Chocolate Sauce

The Plain Vanilla Astrologer's Guide
to the Art of Practicing Astrology

Copyright © 2013 by Pat Geisler
All rights reserved.

No part of this book may be reproduced or used in any form or by any means—
graphic, electronic or mechanical, including photocopying, mimeographing,
recording, taping or information storage and retrieval systems—without written
permission from the publisher. A reviewer may quote brief passages.

by Pat Geisler

Cover and book design by Maria Kay Simms

Library of Congress Control Number 2013938706

International Standard Book Number: 978-1-934976-47-0

Published by ACS Publications,
an imprint of Starcrafts LLC
334-A Calef Highway, Epping, NH 03042
http://www.acspublications.com
http://www.starcraftspublishing.com
http://www.astrocom.com

Printed in the United States of America

TABLE OF CONTENTS

The Plain Vanilla Astrologer's Guide to the Art of Practicing Astrology

Professional DOs and DON'Ts

1 — Ten Rules for Astrologers 1
2 — Ethics of Astrology 3
3 — Starting an Astrology Business 7
4 — Professional Astrology and Money: Keeping Good Records 11
5 — A Little More about Fees 13
6 — Training to be a Professional 16
7 — Astrology Careers 18
8 — "Selling" Astrology 22
9 — "I know just what you should do." 23
10 — Astrological Techniques 25
11 — Listening: You Don't Have to Predict 32
12 — When Your Client Arrives 33
13 — Who Are Your Clients? 35
14 — Predicting Death 37
15 — Planetary Amulets 39
16 — Helping Your Children 41
17 — Condense Your Readings 43
18 — Giving Bad News 46
19 — Dangerous Computers 48
20 — The Matter of Referrals 50
21 — When Your Clients Leave 51
22 — The Apple Tree 53
     About the Author 56

Some of this material has previously appeared elsewhere. The articles on *Astrological Ethics* and *Ten Rules for Astrologers* have been printed on *www.zodiacal.com*. The newsletter of AFAN, the Association for Astrological Networking has also printed some of the articles on *The Professional Astrologer.*

This is a series of rules that I created as a baseline for people who want to do serious astrology. It turned out to be a good start for those who wanted to go beyond serious astrology and into the professional areas. My first rule has been picked up and quoted by many more people than I realized when I first compiled it. This book is for them.

Chapter 1

Ten Rules for Astrologers

One of the problems every student in astrology runs into is why I have always taught one rule first. Every class and every student needs to know it. It is astrology's fundamental basic, rock-bottom principle. Ready?

Here it is—the biggie—write it on your forehead in big gold letters:

EVERYTHING MODIFIES EVERYTHING ELSE.

In order to learn astrology you have to learn how planets and signs function as if they were there all by their lonesome. When you learn a little more, you realize that they almost never are all by themselves, but linked in such a way that they affect each other. Thus:

1. Everything modifies everything else.
2. Nothing is as good or as bad as you think it will be.
3. Forecast conservatively--it's better than looking like a complete fool when you're half wrong.
4. Study love, money and health issues. If you become a professional, 99 percent of your clients will want information on them. If you stay an amateur, it's probably what you want to know. The rest is frosting.
5. Don't take your transits too much to heart. The word transit means "passing on by." The stations are the more reliable indicators.
6. Continue to study. Pay attention to the old timers. They're the ones who taught the astrologers that you think are so wonderful.
7. Take astrology seriously. Don't give away what you know too cheaply. It cost you plenty to learn it. Charge a fair price if you charge.

8. Keep your mouth shut. Don't talk about what your clients tell you and what is confidential information. Before long, nobody will tell you anything and you will stop learning.

9. Listen. Half the time your clients just need somebody to talk to. Most of them will solve their own problems if they get a little moral support from you. They probably don't need a forecast as much as the hand holding.

10. Share what you know with others trying to learn. It keeps astrology vital into the future. It is your gift to the world.

These aren't the only rules, just a few of the big ones.

Chapter 2

Ethics of Astrology

Is there a code of ethics for the astrologer?

Of course. In fact, there are several.

Do you have to follow any of them?

No.

But if you don't follow some sort of ethical code,
you will self-destruct, or your practice will.

**The first rule for the astrologer who offers professional services is privacy.
What the client tells you in confidence is confidential.**

The above rule sounds simple, but a lot of people tend to blurt out bits and pieces of what they know if they don't take active steps to remind themselves continually that this matter is **not** public information.

Everyone has the right to the privacy of their own birth data if they wish. Always ask the client if you may use their data (for a classroom illustration, perhaps, or a lecture topic). If you do use the client's chart, don't put their name on the data and and make sure that some details of their lives are obscured to protect them.

Granted, if you are using data of a public person, such as Madonna or Barack Obama, you don't need to be so picky, but private people have a right to be private.

U.S. courts have ruled on several occasions that newspapers, for instance, can print almost any information and criticism of public figures, but private individuals are another matter altogether. The same rules do not apply to them and woe betide one who holds a private person up to ridicule.

Does this mean that you, as an astrologer, can never discuss what you have learned? I don't think so—not entirely. Most astrologers know that Gemini rules things that come in twos. Some may know that Pisces deals with things that come in threes. I once had a client with Venus in Pisces and she had three functioning kidneys. Venus, of course, rules the kidneys. This was a wonderful bit of evidentiary material which I have shared with other astrologers and astrology students on several occasions. Telling that does not violate privacy, I believe, but I certainly would ***never*** identify her, or use her birth data or her full chart without her permission.

The second rule — or perhaps it should be the first rule — is the golden rule: Treat a client the way you want to be treated.

It sounds simple and it is. But in practice, we sometimes need to assess where we are on this one. Many times parents want the charts of their children analyzed. This is a fair request. However, adult children have a right to their own privacy. Even teenagers should not have information from their charts revealed in ways that would violate that right. Analyzing personality is one thing, discussing sex lives, for instance, is another.

Don't ever give anyone information they are not entitled to because you've seen it in a birth chart. **Just because you see it doesn't mean you have to say it.**

If you question whether an information request is valid, ask yourself how you would take it if your mother or father or whoever had asked about you. Sometimes, in the case of parents, you walk a fine line. Sorry, but it goes with the territory.

For instance, if the parent already knows the child is gay, and they want to know if that child will ever find lasting happiness with a partner, it's a loving concern and a legitimate question, to my mind. But don't break the gay news to parents. This is ***not*** your role.

If the child is handicapped and/or disabled, the parent may ask more probing questions and that's only to be expected. They have a vested interest in knowing whether their child will be self-supporting, or whether custodial care might be needed.

One grandmother I know hesitated to tell her son that she thought his child needed psychiatric care. I looked at the child's chart and encouraged her to speak up, because I told her it appeared that the father was not seeing the problem clearly.

We should always see our role as fostering understanding and helping people make good decisions for themselves. We should be careful not to try to sell our own point of view, however, but rather to offer information and provide an objective sounding board. Sometimes that means being a listener. Not every client wants or needs a full reading. Sometimes they want hand-holding, and just to unburden themselves. It's a valid need and we may be exactly right to serve that need. It is not unethical to charge the full rate for our session, even though we haven't forecast a thing.

One of our greatest roles is peace maker. As astrologers we can see both sides of a conflict between two people and often help them to grasp what is preventing harmony between them. We should never adopt any adversarial stance when we read a chart, however. We are not on anyone's "side." It is not, therefore, a conflict of interest to be an astrologer serving both husband and wife who are not getting along. On the contrary, we may be the only one who can help them see the other point of view. By holding up a "mirror" so they can recognize themselves, we may help clients see what their needs are and how best to deal with their own lives.

But lest we delude ourselves with self-importance, convinced that astrology bestows godlike power or insight, I must mention referrals. Many cases that land on astrologers' laps don't belong there. The client obviously— and sometimes desperately—needs to see an attorney, or a physician, or a psychiatrist or a marriage counselor. If you are truly doing your job, you will send them there.

And if you do, don't meddle with the situation afterwards. I once had a very ill client whom I convinced to see a doctor. He promptly put her in the hospital for tests before doing surgery on the cancer that threatened her life. While she was in the hospital she called me to check on whether it was a good day for a particular test. I refused to say. I told her she was in the doctor's hands and she should do what the doctor said. I am not medically trained, the case was out of my hands and I absolutely will not get in the middle between a patient or client and the professional being consulted.

And this brings up another important principle: understand your limitations. If you don't know anything about investing, don't give investment advice. Every astrologer does not know everything. There are astrologers who specialize in the market. Use them. I sent a client of mine to one last year. I hope she helped him. It is perfectly all right to tell the client, "I don't know." Another thing it is all right to say is, "I'm not sure."

Tell the truth. Sometimes it might be easier to give a client a well-buttered platitude, but you are not doing your job. **Use tact in what you say**. A wise man once told me you could tell people absolutely anything if you knew how to do it. He was right. If you don't know how, take a course in communications, or counseling.

Honesty is always the best thing to bring to the relationship you have with a client. I can see if a husband is ill in the wife's chart. I can't always tell her what he's ill with. I may have to say, "I don't know." This is her chart, not his. When you explain it, people understand quite well.

One time a client was upset with me because her husband died the day after I had done a reading of her chart and she felt I hadn't warned her about it. I had told her there was a health problem and suggested she urge him to get a physical check up. All I could say to her later was that I was sorry my suggestion came too late. I don't run the universe, I simply try to help people make sense of it.

Read conservatively. If something is shown in a chart in three different ways, you can feel confident about a forecast. But things are seldom as good or as bad as you think they will be. Give yourself some leeway. Try to avoid situations where your reading may be compromised. It's very hard to be detached about your own children's lives, sometimes. Send your child to an astrologer you trust for career help if you realize you are looking through rose-colored glasses every time you pick up his or her chart.

The same principle may apply to other relatives and sometimes close friends. If you can't be objective, say so. Sometimes you have to give yourself a good boot in the rear end when you fail to understand your limitations.

The Hippocratic rule physicians follow is a good one for all astrologers to follow: **First, do no harm.** Help if you can. Hands off if you can't. This seems so common sense that we should all realize it, but many times we wade in on someone's life without sufficient forethought.

Prepare thoroughly for each reading. Do the best work you know how to do. It is perfectly acceptable, however, to limit the number of techniques you apply to each client's chart. Back in the pre-computer days, I spent many hours on the mathematics of each chart, double checking constantly. Now preparation time is much faster and we can use more tools, but we do not necessarily see more. Try not to get lost in the details. Stick to reliable techniques and perfect them.

Before you read for any person, take a few moments for meditation or prayer. If you do not wish to call it prayer, call it centering yourself, or whatever you like, but take those moments for quiet, reflective preparation.

Don't try to overload the client with information during each reading. There are many times in life when leaving things out of the reading means that more currently relevant things will fit into it. If you haven't discussed every house in the chart, perhaps it is because you were doing a few of them more intensely. Do this with confidence. Trust yourself. Follow your instincts. Listen to what the client needs.

Of course, sometimes you will be flat out wrong. Admit it. Baseball players get paid big bucks for hitting balls less than a third of the time. Astrologers with only 90 percent batting averages should be worth millions, right?

Sometimes you will fail. Forgive yourself. Try harder next time. Sometimes you will be criticized. Listen carefully. Your enemies will tell you more important things you need to know than your friends ever will.

Charge a fair price. Don't undervalue what you have to give. You worked hard to learn to be an astrologer. Establish your fees and stick to them. Charge when clients call during the year seeking additional information. If you include such calls-or one of them, perhaps-as part of your annual service, make that clear in the beginning.

If a client becomes a friend, make sure the friendship is not simply a camouflaged way to get free information. If in doubt, stop talking astrology with them and see how well the friendship does. It is not unethical to avoid being used. If a client is taking advantage of your good will and demanding increasing amounts of time, increase your fees.

Establish private time. Make sure regular clients who call frequently understand that you don't work on Sundays, for instance. If you have a client so self-centered they constantly intrude on your life over a long period of time (not simply during a crisis), ask yourself if their business is worth it. Listen to your answer.

Don't allow clients to become too dependent. Some people are born leaners. You are not being a good astrologer to allow it. You may have to cut them loose, even if you lose some income.

Don't operate in a vacuum. Talk to other astrologers. Find one you can confide in who will talk honestly with you.

Continue to study. Grow in your knowledge. Learn new techniques. Add to your library. Stretch yourself. Do the best you can to be a better astrologer year by year.

A word about money. Keep good records. Pay your taxes. Don't play "under the table money" games. Hold your head up. If a disgruntled client starts trouble for you, your hands will be clean. Remember, this is your livelihood, not a hobby. Treat it respectfully.

If you are an astrologer, treasure the name and carry it with dignity. Give astrology the best you can. You have some of the knowledge of the universe in your hands. Hold it with great care. It is a trust.

Share what you know. Teach others who ask, help the beginners, counsel those who want to follow in your footsteps. This is your gift to the world.

Chapter 3

Starting an Astrology Business

Starting one's business as an astrologer is not always a planned thing. Most of us do it when the first person offers to pay us to read a chart. It's only later that we begin to consider it our "business."

Some people see astrology as merely a way to make a few dollars "under the table." If this is your approach, then you can probably quit reading about here. You don't want to know what I'm going to talk about anyway.

A real professional who wants to start a business has to see the practice of astrology as a viable way to make a living. Sometimes this happens over a period of time as customers begin banging on your door. Other times, it is a planned decision settled on long ago. Sometimes a very clever astrologer will actually do an election chart on when to get started. But sooner or later you begin to think of it as your occupation. Once you see it as that, you realize you need to get a little organized.

The first thing to do is find out if there are any legal problems with offering consultation services in your community. Some towns have rules against "fortune tellers" and may try to include the practice of astrology in the ordinance. If your town is one of them, you need to be in touch with AFAN's Legal Information committee. Many ordinances have fallen when challenged by AFAN.

Most localities have no restrictions whatever and you have nothing to worry about. A very few insist on a license to operate. Check for this at city hall. Some communities require you to have a vendor's license. You may have to have one if you sell tapes or books. If you do that, be sure to check with your state bureau of taxation for tax forms, particularly if you live in a state that imposes a sales tax. You can probably do some of this work online.

However, most consulting businesses do not require any of this. All you are "selling" is your advice or opinion. You will have to pay income tax, of course, but that's only after you make some income.

The next thing you need is a stack of business cards. Now you may not think this is that high on the priority list, but it is, believe me. Every single client you have should be given a card. Everyone you meet should get one. Your cards help establish you as a legitimate member of the business fraternity, they provide instant recognition and referral possibilities and are your best and cheapest form of advertising as well. People keep them forever. I have had clients call me 15 years after a reading for a new update because they "stumbled on" my old card in their desk somewhere.

Go to a good printer, get 500 cards printed and think carefully about the image you want to present on them. Keep the message simple, use a standard size and format and start with plain white cards. Your name is the most important piece of information on it. Next is your address and phone number. Later on if you really want to get crazy, go for it, but in the beginning, keep it simple. This is not an optional expenditure. If you don't care enough about a business to at least have a business card, you don't care enough. Go sell cars.

I assume you have a base of operations and a telephone. Most astrologers operate out of their homes and use their home telephone, at least in the beginning. If you plan to open an office, of course, do that before you print the cards so you can put the proper address and phone number on the cards. (Duh!)

Get a good answering machine. You don't want to lose out on business if you are taking out the trash or walking the dog. Keep it on all the time. The other option is to use a cell phone and carry it with you at all times.

Buy a good appointment book. You will need it. It will, in fact, become your "bible." You can use it to keep track of your income as well as the appointments. Save all the receipts for any money you spend, by the way. You'll need them come tax time.

Next, you should set up your office. This is a specific room or portion of a room which will be used exclusively for astrology consultations. You need to equip it with your books, your desk, your consulting table and some chairs. You will need some filing cabinets. Get inexpensive ones in the beginning and upgrade later if necessary, but get some right away. At least one.

You will need certain types of supplies. I assume you have a computer for doing chart work. Equip your printer with good quality paper for charts and make sure your name is on them so that if you give your client a copy of the chart, the chart contains the same information that is on your business card. This will be important if you offer a chart service for people who don't have computers but who do astrology or study it. A chart service is a good way to help defray costs of your computer. Keep it in mind.

If you don't have a computer, at least get professional looking chart blanks, either purchased or printed by the company that does your business cards. It's always a good idea to become a "regular" at a business near you that offers good service for anything you do regularly. It pays off in many ways as the years go by. They begin to know you and will sometimes suggest things to you that will be helpful but which might not have occurred to you. They will think of you as "their" customer, and often give your business more attention, watching out for you and even catching your mistakes. Sometimes they will send you clients.

Get some "scratch pads" and pencils and a good sharpener or some pens for both you and your clients to use for notes. Make sure you have a dish of some type in which you can put some of your cards for your clients to take.

Get folding files that you can label with the names of your clients. I have a simple rule I have used for years. The first time I do a chart, I do not put it in a file folder, but merely in the filing cabinet. If the client comes again the following year, I start a file folder with information on the date of the client's appointments and the fee charged. This automatically sorts my clients into "one-night-stands" and repeaters. It also saves space and file folders.Keep a special file for the charts of people who made appointments for consultations and never kept them. Check it regularly. Sometimes they will call back because they just forgot and it will save you work if the chart is already done. Sometimes they will make a second appointment and "forget" that one, too. It pays to know who they are.

Keep a record of people whose checks for readings bounce. Note it on their charts. If they make good on the check, then read for them again, if you wish, but I always ask for cash the next time.

Some astrologers will include a lot of notes on their readings and predictions in the file folders. I don't particularly recommend this unless you live alone. The practice leaves too much personal information available to anyone who may pry into your files. However, many astrologers do so and don't worry about it.

If you do any special work of any sort, particularly rectification, keep all your notes and worksheets. You may need them later. Don't throw anything away that is verification data for the birth time.

Do you plan to offer recording service for your readings? If so, you will need a good, reliable recorder and a supply of tapes or CDs, which you can usually get cheaply at any good electronics store. Add the cost to your readings.

Many astrologers leave recording up to the client if they feel comfortable about having the reading recorded. If you want to allow it, make sure a plug is near your consulting table for your clients to use.

A word about tax matters. These refer to the United States., of course, since I am unfamiliar with tax laws in other countries. Initially you may practice only as a consultant and you can file income taxes simply as a consultant. That entitles you to business deductions. Your business is technically a "sole proprietorship." Even if you teach or lecture or offer private tutoring, all payments for these serivces can still funnel into the sole proprietorship classification

Later on you might decide, for various reasons, to incorporate. Go online to the state bureau of incorporation in your state capitol and get information and forms to do this. State laws vary widely. There is usually someone who will answer your questions on an 800 line or an ombudsman. They will send you brochures and general information as well. Take advantage of this if it is available. It will save you money.

Most state governments have web sites now with all the information you need readily available. Crank up your search engine and find out what you need to know.

Consult an attorney only if all else fails. If you MUST consult an attorney, look for one who offers a special price on an initial consultation. Sometimes a 15 minute session will answer your questions and you might as well get it as cheaply as you can.

Now let's talk about fees and advertising. The best possible advertising you can have is word-of-mouth. There is only one way to get it. You have to let people know you are an astrologer and you have to provide good service when they come to you. Decide in advance how much service a fee for the first reading buys.

If a client has a question about their reading and calls within a couple of weeks after it I think that question should be answered without charge. If a client has a single question about some forecast during the year, I will answer that without charge. But if a client has a lot of questions, they obviously need a secondary consultation mid-year and that should be set up with a reduced or hourly fee, in my opinion.

Decide on how much work an initial consultation involves. I use a standard natal plus one year's progression plus solar return. The following year I do the same thing. Obviously subsequent years' consultations put more emphasis on the forecasting than the first year but I keep the consultation fee the same.

If there are other professional astrologers near you and you know their fees, it will give you a clue as to where to position yourself. Charge less in the beginning. Don't set a fee at the same rate as somebody who's been doing it for 20 years. People love a bargain.

Once you have decided on what service you offer, you may want to print up a small brochure of your fees and make it available to clients. This is not a must, but you should at least have an idea of what you want to charge and what you want that fee to cover so you aren't caught by surprise when people ask you to do a chart comparison, for instance.

Another way to set your fee is to figure out how much time an average chart takes to prepare and to read and set a price on your time. Don't be afraid to ask a decent amount. People don't appreciate what they get too cheaply.

You can always raise your fees, but in the beginning, don't overdo it. Keep in mind that if this is going to be a business to you, you want to bring your clients back again. A barber who shaves every customer bald may get all the hair the first time, but he won't get much repeat business as a stylist.

How much or how little advertising you choose to do is up to you. In the beginning, you may see it as a costly expense and put it aside for later. That's why I said to get the cards first. They will at least get you started.

There are always opportunities to pay for advertising in programs and brochures at astrological conventions and the like. But in the beginning of your business, you should look for ways to get attention free. Most of your clients will never go to an astrological convention.

Talk pleasantly to everyone you meet. You are your own best advertising medium and everyone will judge all astrologers by you. Smile a lot. Be polite and courteous and don't pick fights with strangers. Listen to people when they talk to you. Don't try to sell astrology to people who don't "believe" in it or argue with them over it and never –I mean never, never, NEVER—offer astrological advice when you are not asked for it. If this is a tough order, you aren't ready to be a consultant.

Now, a quick word here about qualification. Back in the dark ages, astrologers had no such thing as certification. Today many astrological groups offer it. It's a very good idea to go for the tests with one of the larger organizations and earn certification. It will do two very important things for you: prove to you that you know what you're doing and prove to your clients that you have the skills that meet the standards of your peers. These are good things.

Now that you are ready to launch your life as a professional astrologer, a few closing words are in order. Continue your education. Subscribe to as many astrological publications as you can afford, study as much as you have time for and join some professional organizations. These will keep you up to date and offer opportunities for professional friendships. You will appreciate them as the years go by.

Oh, and take a picture of yourself. In later years it will help to remember how young you looked when you started out. You'll feel better about how much you've learned and how far you've come since then.

Bon voyage!

Chapter 4

Professional Astrology and Money Keeping Good Records

If you are doing astrology for money you need to know how much you are making. Not only will it help you plan for your professional future, but it makes it easier to do your tax returns. You ARE reporting all your income, aren't you? If you aren't, you can get in trouble with the government, to say nothing of the bad karma involved.

The first thing you need is some sort of record system. Get a book in which you can keep track of things. If it happens to be the same book in which you keep track of appointments, fine. If it's a separate book, that works, too. This is not rocket science, just housekeeping. Write down the date and the amount earned for each conference and phone call and lecture and lesson. Do it as you go. At the end of each month you can make a note on the total.

There, that wasn't so bad, was it? This will be a big help when you see your tax preparer next year.

Next comes the expenses. These you get to deduct so you don't have to pay too much income tax. This is good stuff, so pay attention. You can deduct part of all your household expenses if you read for clients in your home. The key thing is to have a set "office area" that you keep for astrology. (This is the law, by the way.) The computer you use, the chairs you and your clients sit in, the books you put on your astrological shelves and even the paper you use for chart blanks are ALL deductible. It's wonderful!

Save every little receipt for anything you buy or do for your office. New curtains? Deductible. New computer program? Deductible. Ink cartridges for the chart printer? Deductible. This is all stuff that comes under expenses.

Get a large file or big envelope and put into it all your phone bills (part or all deductible), your receipts for purchases, your heat and air-conditioning bills (part will be deductible), etc. **If in doubt, save it.** Don't forget your bill for the price of professional journals, your memberships in astrological organizations, and oh, my gosh—remember to keep track of the MILEAGE. When you have some, write it down. Don't wait until next

March when the tax man or woman asks about it. That's too late. What did you use mileage for? Visiting astrology groups, going to lectures, traveling to class sites, etc.

Save your convention bills. Save the charges for meals at the hotels where you stayed, or any other kind of meal. If you charged these things, save your Visa or MasterCard bill. A convention is a wonderful thing because it is completely deductible in the year you attend.

Some things are not completely deductible each year. If you buy a new computer, for instance, your tax person may suggest writing off the expense over three or four years to give you the best shot at reducing taxes. This can be a big help in a year where you have fewer deductions and more income.

Many of us write checks for our expenses. Your check register is a gold mine of deductions if you forgot to write something down. There you will find a nice little canceled check which proves you paid for something.

Use your check register wisely. One handy way is to "code" anything that will be an astrological practice deduction. Maybe you will want to keep a green pen, or a purple one and put a tiny asterisk or a mark by each check for something that you want to note come tax time. Or, simply write "astrological" beside the listing.

If your practice is big enough to have a separate checking account, that's wonderful. Your job is easier. But sooner or later you will use your personal account for something when the other check register isn't handy and this will alert you to it a year from now when you would otherwise have forgotten it. It's one thing to forget to write down the fee you charged for that midnight phone call. It's another to forget a deduction.

When tax time comes, you're all set. You have a complete list of income and a fat file of deductions.

Under U.S. law, a self-employed person must show a profit once in a while, like three out of every five years. It doesn't have to be a large profit. One dollar will do. That gives you a lot of leeway. If your practice appears to be losing money, you still have to file an income tax return.

But if you are losing too much money maybe you aren't charging enough for your services. At this point you need to sit down and have a good talk with yourself. Is this a part time or a full time occupation? Is it worth your time or isn't it? Do you deliver something of value or not?

Add up the hours you put into each chart, or lesson, or lecture. Figure out what you're actually earning per hour. It's usually a shock. Then rethink your fees.

If you want your practice to grow, you might consider advertising. How much, what kind and the type of image you want to maintain are all part of the "money picture" you need. And don't forget—advertising is deductible, too.

Now, if you have gotten this far and you already know all this stuff and have a good system for keeping records and are making a decent living in astrology, you have chosen to be among the true professionals. Hold your head high and be proud of yourself. You've earned it.

Chapter 5

A Little More about Fees

You are in a service business, remember. If you screw it up, you will be the only one to suffer. Get the money part down and then forget it. Feel free to break all the rules. I do. But at least I have some rules. You need some, too.

Step No. 1

Sit down with a piece of paper and decide in advance what you want to charge for each type of work. Feel free to ask around for other astrologers' fees. If you are in an urban environment, charge a ton or people won't respect you. If you want to help kids and people without a lot of money, charge less. If you live in a small town, you'll probably want to charge less.

In my opinion you should never do *pro bono* work except for the 100 percent family discount. Astrology is not a necessity like bread and butter. It is a luxury. People pay for their luxuries. If you choose to do a free chart for somebody, be well aware that you are giving them a costly luxury for nothing.

There are astrologers who will disagree with me on the above. They like to have a sliding rule for payment and if they feel sorry for someone in a difficult situation, may charge half fees. I think that point of view is a copout, and I don't do cut-rate astrology. Either charge your full rate or give it away.

There will be a cost to you to give it away however. One old astrologer told me people do not appreciate or respect what they get too cheaply or for free. It's true. I saw how that worked a long time ago so I don't do it.

But do plot it all out. Set a base rate for a natal analysis with year-ahead forecast. Add half again if you are doing a chart comparison. (that's two charts, so double the analysis fee and include no forecasting, so it's fair. Charge double for elections. Charge triple for business work. (such as when to start it, etc.) Charge half of your base rate for a consultation of say, a half hour or 3/4 hour between annual forecasts, where you don't have to redo the chart. Charge a quarter or a third of your base rate for a phone call with one problem. If it gets into more than 10 minutes, schedule a consultation.

If two people want a chart comparison and forecasting, figure out how much additional you want to add.

What I've just given to you are suggestions. Think out your own set of appropriate fees. Write them down. Decide how you want to be paid. Cash only? Accept personal checks? Write that down, too.

Step 2
Design a small one-sheet-of-paper brochure or list of fees. Explain what the fees cover. If you offer any free services (such as the first phone call about a single question between annual chart updates). Add that.

Step 3
When your client makes the appointment tell the client what your fee for the work is. When the client comes to see you, give every one of them your card and a copy of your brochure.

Step 4
Don't sweat it. They expect to pay. Ask them, if they start to leave and have forgotten it. It just means you have so fascinated them that they have gotten too absorbed. It is a compliment to you. They will probably be more embarassed than you that they forgot.

Step 5
Pat them on the back as they go out the door and tell them you'll see them next year. Wish them a good year. Repeat business is what keeps the astrologer in business.

One more thing, do only as much work per day as you feel you can do comfortably. Otherwise you risk burning yourself out and not doing as good a job as you might.

Frankly, I notice that astrologers who say they do—or can do—many readings per day either have air Suns or fire Suns, but they aren't water people like me. Air Suns are super detached and fire types have the energy to burn. But when you have water energy, there is a big limit on how much you can do. Pace yourself. Even earth Sun folks can do more than water types. But I doubt that it is all due to the Sun sign. I'm sure the Ascendant, Moon and planetary arrangement are also part of it. If there is a lot of water in the chart, though, I know there is a sharp limit.

Step 6
Be sure you are charging a realistic price for your labors. Many altruistic types become astrologers and charge too little. There is a strong compassion factor at work when a client is in need. But that is not always the best option.

Back in the very early 1970s I was helping to run a drop-in center for young drug abusers and because I was an astrologer, a lot of them would talk to me about their troubles. I didn't charge them, of course.

I told one young man that he was in imminent danger of being busted as a dealer unless he cleaned up his act. I liked him a lot—he had a chart formed around a beautiful grand trine—and I was worried about him.

(For those who ask, too soft a chart is usually worrisome because these are people who take the easy way out when times get tough. His was a very soft chart.)

He took my advice and had divested himself of all his drugs when he was stopped and searched. After that, however, it wasn't long before he went back to dealing when he needed a few bucks. Soon, it was a bigger business than ever.

A couple of years later he was in prison.

He later asked me to read for him again and I told him that if I did, I would charge him a whole lot of money, so he would pay more attention to what I told him. He never came for the reading until 30 years later.

That old astrologer who had told me never to give knowledge or readings free said it was like casting pearls before swine. People only appreciate what they pay for and their appreciation is often in direct proportion to what it cost them.

I never forgot the lesson I learned from that client who was a drug dealer, and I must say there are times when I want to raise my fees to $10,000 so people will pay attention. I don't, but sometimes I think we charge too little for what has cost us years of time and money to learn.

Chapter 6

Training to be a Professional

Some years ago I taught classes on astrology at the local community college and one of the students in my beginning course said she wanted to get through the three courses I offered as fast as possible since she wanted to be a professional astrologer. She told me it looked like a good way to make a living.

Long before the three courses were over, she told me she thought it would take her a bit longer to be ready to do it professionally because there was so much to learn. She attended classes a few more years, as a matter of fact, but to date has still never become professional. The more she found out, the more worried she became about the responsibility she would be taking on.

I think it is wonderful to be learning astrology. I think it is great some of you are already thinking in terms of making this your life work. But --there's always a "but," isn't there? The problem is taking money for what you do. Once you do that, you tell the world you know what you're doing and you can handle the karmic load that comes along with offering to tamper with someone's life. That is a heavy thing.

As long as you have "amateur" status--meaning, you don't take money--you can read all the charts you like for as many people as you like and get them to tell you how you're doing with accuracy and offer as much counsel as you want to—and it is all part of the learning process. If you are in college and studying psychology, it can add richness to your knowledge.

I, too, am a self-taught astrologer. I spent many, many hours hunched over the math calculations in the days before computers. You can attain a high degree of accuracy that way if you work on it. I did, and it was hard work, but worth it.

The way I "trained" was to do just what I suggest you do: read for tons of people you don't know or don't know well. Tell them you are learning, get them to give you good feedback and consider yourself well paid with that knowledge. Don't take money yet. It took me 10 years of study to get around to that.

Give yourself time to learn your craft well. Astrology is a craft in a sense that it can be learned by anyone who devotes time and effort to the learning. Yes, some of us have a better feel for it than others, but anyone can learn.

You wouldn't eat pizza with bread that is half cooked. A good astrologer takes a bit of time to season, in my opinion. Find a few teachers--try them all. If you really want to learn, you will learn from everybody in the field. Then take a test from one of the big organizations that offer them. That will help you see what you know and where there are any holes in your education.

When you are ready to be a "professional" it will be to start a career you can take pride in and approach with a sense of responsibility and satisfaction. It is a wonderful thing to be able to help people. But the doctor who takes up a scalpel before he is ready can also hurt. And that's the first rule in medicine: "First, do no harm." It's a good one for our profession, too.

An old astrologer I knew when I first started doing charts in the early 70s told me to focus on love, money and health issues because that's what most of your clients really want to know. So I can't claim the advice is original.

Besides, if the rare occasional oddball actually asks you about their spiritual purpose in life or the meaning of their Jupiter-Saturn square it will come as a delightful surprise and you won't swamp them with rhetoric when you answer.

As a teacher, I have to remember my dad's first advice about talking too much: The mind can only absorb what the seat can endure. That goes double for clients.

Confidentiality is a must and I take it seriously. I grew up a Catholic, a religion in which priests vow to keep forever private whatever is told to them in confession. I am also a retired journalist, and many journalists have gone to prison over the issue of confidentiality and some have died .

As an astrologer, I have told my clients that what they tell me stays in the room. I don't repeat it. If they couldn't trust me to mean that, they wouldn't feel comfortable pouring out their heart, telling me about their pains, their fears, their griefs.

If someone asked me for a good day to commit a murder, I wouldn't do that kind of astrology. There is no good day for that. If someone who asks for a reading is a drug dealer and is open with me, I would counsel him or her against such a career choice (this actually happened to me), but I wouldn't tell anyone else. Their choices will boomerang on them without my aid. (the dealer in question was later busted and spent many years in prison). **This is the deal: I take your money, I keep your secrets. It's an implied contract.**

We make many such implicit contracts in our lives. Take the one many of us make with employers: I give you a fair day's work for a fair day's pay. Or the deal we make with the TV repair man: You fix my set, I give you money.

These are simple examples, but truth is a simple thing. Integrity is keeping your word. Confidentiality between client and astrologer is vital to both.

Chapter 7

Astrological Careers

There are many kinds of astrologers to be. Not all of them may suit you.

The first and most likely is consultant, of course. That means helping somebody with a problem or to understand themselves or another person with whom they're having difficulty. Maybe it means estimating how long their current problem is going to last, or how it will come out. If you can see a hopeful ending people will be very grateful for the light at the end of the tunnel.

If it's not a hopeful ending, having some warning so as to soften the blow or shift gears is very helpful. Many people like as much warning as possible. Others are frightened by it. Here's where some good judgment comes in. Consultants should have some.

Scorpios and Aries usually want straight answers. Aries wants them without wasting their time, too. Capricorns are sure it's going to be bad anyway so you might as well tell them. Just do it carefully. They don't really like bad news—they just expect it. Air sign people are quite good at planning alternatives so if you can give the Geminis, Libras and Aquarians some hint as to more fertile avenues to explore, they'll face the problem with the mental processes already engaged.

Fire signs like to think of themselves as warriors. Give them a "battle" to fight and they'll gird up and get ready. If they've already been at war with whatever is going on, they may be getting tired and need to learn how to draw on fresh reserves. Help them do that.

Earth and water signs are a bit iffy. Depends on the individual. Cancers will probably cry. Don't worry, most of them have their cry in the beginning, then straighten up and deal with things. Keep the tissues handy, anyway. Pisces is a timid sign to start with so go gently down that road. If it's money and you've got a Taurus, you've got a problem. This is not a flexible sign so you have to suggest alternatives to however they have dealt with problems in the past. Their great strength is simply endurance so they often just outlive the roadblocks. Virgos deal best with anything that they can "fix." Help them find repair tools and instructions books.

In other words, consulting is the art of helping others in whatever way can be most productive and hopeful for a particular person. If you're good with people and want to be of service, you can't beat consulting.

You need some good mathematical skills. These days with the advent of the computer, there is a disinclination to actually do the chart from scratch by oneself, but instead to just punch it up. In my opinion this is a mistake. I think every astrologer needs to learn the basics of chart calculation in order to be sure they have a reliable chart with which to work.

Some astrologers become researchers and that's another place good math ability is invaluable.. If you have intense curiosity, love the process of gathering information and analyzing it to find answers to tough questions (especially ones that no one has solved yet) other astrologers will practically kneel at your feet. Most of us don't have the patience for this job, but an excellent researcher can redirect the whole course of astrology at large with good information carefully shown. It helps to have another source of income, of course. Research takes a lot of time and some of it is a thankless process. Also, it doesn't pay very well.

Teaching is the divine art of sharing what you know. If you have Jupiter strong in your personal chart, you will probably end up with students in one way or another. This is an excellent companion talent for a consultant to have and many of us have it. It's also the reason most of us go to conferences whenever possible. We like the travel, we have friends all over the world and we can learn interesting things in such teaching arenas.

Some witty person once said, "Those who can, do. Those who can't, teach." I think he was jealous. What he should have said was, "Those who can, do. Those can do more, teach." Good teachers are like lights in the dark. They shine enough to help others find the light switches, too. If you find one, pay attention. You never know what bit of information you hear that may prove helpful 20 years from now.

Astrologers who write are part teacher, part consultant. Some of them are researchers. It's one way researchers can earn some money from all that effort they've put in, so it helps if they have some verbal skills to go along with their mathematical comprehension.

Most astrologers, if at all successful, have decent communication skills. Many of them lecture and many write. Some of them aren't particularly good at either but they have tons of information and it pays to listen to them. Some don't know a lot of astrology but they write well. Some of those end up doing Sun-sign stuff for various publications. It's a living.

Occasionally you find truly fine speakers and outstanding writers. They can do a great deal for astrology and others if they use those talents. They might even make a decent wage.

This whole business of money is a crucial one, you know, for a person with career goals in astrology. When I first began in astrology it was a poverty job. It didn't pay much and was mostly done as a labor of love. Movements in the '70s and '80s began to push astrologers to seek a more professional approach to their work and to charge realistic fees for the years of study and work put into acquiring their skills. Some of the poverty mentality still exists, but most astrologers are beginning to get smart about what they used to give away for practically nothing.

Astrology, in many ways, is a luxury item in life. It isn't food or clothing or shoes for the kids. Most human beings will live their whole lives without ever consulting an astrologer. Being able to see ahead a little bit is a luxury. So, it should cost a luxury price, in my opinion. And those who do it, should value what they have, which is a peek at how the universe works and our place in it.

It helps for astrologers to earn good wages. People respect those who 'succeed' in the world, so perhaps the battle of astrology for respect is more financial than anything else.

There are other things astrologers do, of course. Some have specialties of one sort or another. Some study earthquakes or the stock market. Some are "mundane" experts, who work with the charts of nations and are interested in world events and political developments. One friend is an outstanding long-range weather forecaster. Some study the stars (not the planets—the stars). Others look at vast cycles that may affect our lives. All of these specialties may be partly research, part writing, part lecturing, part teaching and part consulting as well. There is no one way to do it. Most astrologers get their fingers in a lot of pies.

Astrologers are a rather distinctive breed. They can be quite prickly about their independence and are happiest carving their own roads in the wilderness. Many will turn their minds to ways to improve their income through astrology rather than taking part in traditional careers when they need money.

A surprising number of astrologers live in small communities without another astrologer in town. The internet and telephones have done wonders to unite astrologers and improve their sociability. Perhaps this is why so many travel, lecture and write.

A final type of astrologer may be one who remains a perennial student. Professional astrologers treasure them. Not everyone wants to take knowledge to the career level. Some of these people run conventions, publish magazines or manage astrology organizations or groups. Some sign up for the classes, or buy the books. Most of them have more knowledge than they give themselves credit for. These are the ones who are the unpaid ambassadors of good will for astrology. Thank heaven for them.

Back to consulting now. It's the most common career in astrology. You'll notice I've mentioned money a few times, but there are other things of equal value that should be addressed.

First is education. No astrologer is worth a nickel who hasn't spent years studying what they want to practice. In other times, astrology was taught as an apprenticeship to an older, experienced astrologer. Many older astrologers today had to educate themselves with the few books then available. Today there are far more resources available to those who want to learn. Take advantage of them if you plan a career in astrology.

Learn from everyone you can. Read as many books as you can cram into your time and ask questions constantly.

Testing is the natural outcome of all this. Today's large astrology organizations have instituted testing programs and rankings. Jump in and take some tests. Learn how much you know and where the holes are in your education. Then go back and fill them in. It's the only way to do it.

Of course there is formal education, too. Kepler College in Washington state offers studies in astrology. The International Academy of Astrology online is offering excellent coursework. There are others. Be sure to cast your net widely for information before deciding what to choose.

Let's not forget the consulting skills themselves. These have become a modern specialty in psychology and it may pay you to take some special classes in it if you can. If you want to be a good astrologer consider it.

For a consulting astrologer, the first thing to learn is how not to talk too much. Let your clients talk. Before an astrologer meets with anyone who seeks a consultation, the individual's chart should be done. You should know what they're coming to talk about—or have an idea, anyway—ahead of time. The position of transiting Saturn is your first clue. It's what the general problem area is in their life right now.

Any eclipses, or planetary stations that have hit their chart recently can tell you about the current difficulty. Mars transits are usually tip-offs to the latest annoyance.

The late, great Evangeline Adams, sometimes called the ''mother of American Astrology,'' used to do a chart for the time any client called for a reading. Some astrologers do one for the time of the consultation. This can be a helpful technique, particularly when there is no known birth time. If you have a timed chart with a decent source for the birth time (A or AA-rated is best) you can probably skip the additional work of doing such charts. Evangeline Adams, however, was working in an era where precise birth times were hard to come by and such event charts were invaluable.

This business about learning to listen to your clients is important. While I suggest you know what is going on, it is always wise to let your clients tell you about it. First of all, they have the key slant on how things are going and it's amazing how many times people come to see astrologers just to talk about their problems. Basically, they want hand-holding.

This is a valid need and many times clients will talk themselves around to a perspective on what they need, and then go and fix whatever is wrong without a bit of help from the astrologer. They didn't need forecasting nearly as much as simple approval or the feeling that they "could" actually deal with their lives. This, too, is part of an astrologer's job.

Don't underestimate the power of your words. Comments I have made about someone's chart have come back to me many years later. Always be aware that what you say has power. Make sure it is helpful, generous and true.

And then we must deal with the maturity issue. I'm not talking years here, but the wisdom that comes from living life with a certain integrity. Clients want to be helped and they expect to find a reasonably detached person who cares about them. It helps to have dealt with your own life issues well.

Don't expect people to see your viewpoint. You should expect to see theirs and help them from where they stand.

My final comment on what an astrologer needs is about ethics. This has become very much more fashionable a topic in modern astrology than it once was. For some of us who have talked about the ethics of knowledge for a long time, it has been gratifying to see our opinions being validated.

Some organizations put more emphasis on it than others, but you should explore ideas on ethics as a preliminary to beginning your career. Know how others deal with the issues that will affect your life—confidentiality, honesty and integrity are your working tools.

Obviously you need to do more than the basic chart and progressions in the beginning. But try not to multiply techniques. Do the ones you know well until you know them better. Add other techniques to help you fill out more details if you like, but if you get too bogged down in minutiae you aren't helping your client and you are wasting your own valuable time.

If none of this daunts you, come on in. The water's fine. You get to share a piece of the universe and how it works as part of your life. That's a pretty big payback.

Chapter 8

"Selling" Astrology

Convincing others of the spiritual comfort of your philosophy is a problem faced by generations of religious missionaries and other spiritual teachers. Most of them thought they were bringing a spiritual light to dark corners of the world and some of them didn't want to dilute that effort by paying attention to any other point of view.

They're entitled to do that. It's not your job to change their ideas. You can't "sell" astrology, either, you can only demonstrate its value.

The wisest quickly realize that when people are hungry or hurting, or grieving, they can't lift their head out of those earthly concerns until someone gives them a meal, or a bandaid, or a shoulder.

No one would have listened to Mother Teresa if she hadn't been feeding the hungry, washing the abandoned and the diseased and giving them a clean and comfortable place to die holding the hand of someone who cared. After she did all that for them, suddenly her message of love for human beings came through loud and clear. She didn't have to say a word.

When we are concerned about the worries and pains of our fellow man—whether they are for love, or money or health or schoolwork or anything else—and do our best to ease those, surely we are doing more to demonstrate our own commitment to a spiritual pathway than anything else we can do. And if our road and our goals are such good ones, we don't need to "sell" them very hard. They are their own attraction.

If you do the simple things people need, when they are ready for more, they will ask. Mother Teresa's motto was, "Do small things with great love."

We should do astrology with love, too.

Chapter 9

"I know just what you should do..."

Hey, what's your Sun sign?

With that introduction, all too many astrology buffs and students may feel free to make a personal comment to the person who responds.

"You're a Gemini? Boy, Saturn is in your Sun sign and you'd better be careful of men. Be sure to get a credit report on any new guys who tell you they have a good offer for you."

"You're a Sag? Bet you're meeting some crooks these days. You'd better stay on the straight and narrow and not go betting with any bookies."

"A Libra? Sure hope you don't live too close to your in-laws, 'cause they don't like you right now. If I were you' I'd just avoid them for a year or two."

The astrologer may continue with more choice bits of advice, as well.

Or perhaps it's a good friend who's having a tough time on the job.

"Well, your career house is getting a Uranus transit. Start looking for another job. You'll need one," says the astrologer over coffee.

The comments may be well-meaning, but they often irritate people who get them, and as a public relations gambit for astrology are certainly counter-productive. Besides, the comments are probably superficial at best, seldom based on the whole chart and in danger of being wrong.

Nobody likes to get unasked-for advice. Nobody likes to get "sold" something in a casual conversation, and nobody likes the feeling that their personal business is fair game. The net result is that they don't like the astrologer and they sure don't like astrology.

We forget that one of the important rules of being a good astrologer is: **Never** (and I mean **never never NEVER**) give advice to someone who hasn't asked for it.

Never give advice without a chart in front of you. Never give advice based on your psychic "hunches" received in a dream last night—unless you say so. And never do it at all unless you are asked.

Many beginners in astrology are so enthused about what they are learning they want to share it with the world, feeling they can help "improve" it, regardless of other people's resistance to "the truth."

Some astrologers are impressed with their own self-importance as members of "those in the know" and can't wait to talk about it.

Some astrologers are just so wrapped up in their craft they aren't paying attention. It doesn't matter why you are giving all that free, unsought advice.

If you have any hope of being a good professional, you need to be a person others trust with their secrets. Blabbermouths with no sense of responsibility are not the first choice when one is looking for a consultant.

And those who offer unsought advice soon get a reputation as a busybody or worse. Help yourself and help astrology: Keep your mouth shut, and your opinions to yourself unless someone says they want to know.

Chapter 10

Astrological Techniques

The Solar Chart

If I don't have a birth time for a client, I use a Solar chart. I use the noon time for all the planets but I plug them into a Sun-rising chart, with equal houses. Today the Sun is in Sagittarius, so the 2nd house will be Capricorn, 3rd Aquarius and so on, with the same degree — the Sun's degree — on each cusp.

The reason I use the noon placements is that no matter what time of day the person is born, the Moon can't be more than about 6 degrees away from it in either direction and the other planets even closer. Obviously there is no way to get the angles, but you can't have everything.

As to transits, yes, they work quite well with the solar chart. Progressions aren't as reliable since the secondary system I use needs to be exact. I don't allow orbs on most progressions. The timing on forecasting, therefore, won't be tight, but it will get you in the ball park. The simple one-degree method will give you quite a good idea of the year's highlights and the New Moons can also help you spot the activation.

If you tell your client that not knowing his birth time hinders you from getting a good prediction, he may or may not want to hunt down his time. That's his choice and I think you have done your part on this one. I've done a lot of charts with no time and it can be quite accurate.

Other times, of course, you fall on your face. But I've found myself in the mud plenty of times, and you just pick yourself up and go on. You can screw up a forecast on a dead accurate chart too, so just chalk it up to a bad day.

And then there are the times you give a smashing analysis on the wrong time altogether and the forecast turns out to be wonderful. The universe is definitely Libra--it likes to keep things evened up, I think.

A "timed" solar is created by taking your natal chart with an accurate time and putting the Sun on the Ascendant and using equal houses of the Sun's degree. It is similar to a regular solar chart, but is a symbolic chart in the sense that it focuses on the Sun, which is the fundamental identity and shows you your life from the solar perspective.

If you wish a timed lunar chart (to see about your childhood influences and your emotional nature, perhaps) you can put your corrected Moon on the Ascendant and use equal houses of that same degree. This would give you a lunar perspective. Of course, this implies you HAVE a correct time.

Many ancient cultures gave the Moon far more importance than the Sun, for instance. We here in the west are accustomed to thinking in terms of "individual" spiritual identity, but there are other lands and other times in which one's function within the clan or the tribe was far more important than what one wanted to do or be as an individual.

You can actually do this with any planet. It's an excellent practice tool if you want to look at a specific planetary influence.

A solar chart is very useful for all astrologers. It acts as a kind of background to predictive work as well as a substitute for the unknown birth time. It is an indispensable tool if you write or forecast for the public, since the public has been trained to think in terms of Sun sign.

A common request is, "I'm a Leo. What does the year look like for Leos?" And all you need is a solar chart for Leo. You will be surprised by how much accuracy you will develop if you use it consistently. Try putting the solar chart with every chart you do for a while and make predictions from it as well as the ones with the correct birth time. It will enhance your work. And probably surprise you.

When You Draw a Blank

It takes time to get the knack of putting a chart together concisely, and sometimes I fail after all the years of doing it. We all have off days even when we know better. But having said that, I know that sometime this year I will look at a chart I have just calculated and think, "Now what in the world does this mean?"

When I sit down to look at a chart and draw a complete blank, I go back to the basics of 1, 2, 3 and it steadies me on the way. If you have the 1, 2, 3 always tucked in your back pocket, it's like money in the bank, something for the rainy days and Mondays. What is 1, 2, 3? Easy—Sun, Moon and Ascendant. By the time you've covered those three things you are going along just fine and the reading will probably proceed as it should.

A handy trick

Here's something I do which sounds simple and it is, but is one of those useful things I can do and I never overlook its value. At the beginning of every year, I sit down with a 3 x 5 index card and the ephemeris for the year and make a list of each planet's stations, both retrograde and direct, the degree at which each occurs and the dates. I also note the eclipses. My card will look something like this:

**Mercury: SR Feb. 22, 4 Pisces, SD March 15,
20 Aquarius. Venus: SR etc. Jupiter SD, etc.**

Then you also make a list of the eclipses for the year:

**Sun, total, 17 Taurus, and the date,
Moon partial, 5 Scorpio and the date, and so on.**

You stick that little card in your ephemeris and you keep it there all year. Every time you do a chart, you take it out and check the things that hit this client's chart.

After you do this a few years you will notice something very interesting. A lot of degrees that are in for action during the year will have stations of more than one planet as well as eclipses and New or Full Moons at the same degree or nearly so. For instance, Mercury will station at 22 Aries and you notice that there is a Saturn station at 22 Libra and a solar eclipse at 21 Cancer. There is also a lunar eclipse at say 19 Cap. And both the Aries and Libra New Moons are in the late teens.

Now, it doesn't require a lot of fancy math to realize that any chart with placements in the 19-22 degree cardinal range is going to be affected in a pronounced way at the time of the stations, or the eclipses.

When it comes to planetary transits, the stations are powerful indicators. Every year there is some major planetary activity that dominates. One year it may be a triple conjunction of Uranus and Pluto as they go retrograde and direct, passing and re-passing each other. Another year Jupiter and Saturn repeat a series of squares, etc. Notice the degrees at which the direction changes. Those degrees should be listed on your card. They are important for that year.

Next year, do this again. Watch how the degrees of the stations are echoed by New Moons and Full Moons close to or on those activated areas as the year goes by. Sometimes they are all in cardinal or fixed. Occasionally they may be all in fire, or water. Watch these linkages shape up. If any chart has these areas of the zodiac occupied by planets, that chart will be in for the action. If the degrees getting emphasis are on the angles, major activity is scheduled.

Ordinary transits, no matter how impressive, do not produce events as regularly as stations on specific areas of the chart. If Mercury is active in the chart this year, making and receiving a lot of aspects, for instance, then a Mercury station near progressed or natal Mercury can set off events. The same is true of Venus, or Jupiter or Saturn.

The solar system is like a game of tag, and sometimes the one who is "It" changes, bouncing from planet to planet. Your little card just helps you keep "score."

Solstice Points

Solstice points seem mysterious if you don't have a good visual idea of how they work. When you understand them, they can provide secondary readings to planetary positions and often illuminate much that is otherwise hidden.

To start with, visualize a large rubber band with the signs of the zodiac on it. Every degree is clearly marked. Put a nail in a table through the 0 Cancer point. That's the summer solstice.

Stretch the rubber band and when you get to the 0 Capricorn point, nail that end down. Now you have the rubber band stretched between two points—the two solstices of the year.

Now look at where Pisces is. It will be opposite the Libra degrees. The Aries degrees will be opposite the Virgo ones. 29 Gemini will be opposite 1 Cancer. 28 Gemini will be opposite 2 Cancer. 29 Sagittarius will be opposite 1 Capricorn. 27 Sagittarius will be opposite 3 Capricorn. 15 Taurus is opposite 15 Leo and 15 Scorpio is opposite 15 Aquarius. 26 Sag is opposite 4 Capricorn.

The only triplicity that lines up is the fixed one—all the cardinal signs have a solstice point in mutable and all the mutables have their solstice points in cardinal.

This is where you can see clearly the potency of the fixed signs, since all fixed signs reflect back to other fixed signs. Solstice points are sometimes called "reflex points" or antiscia because it seems as if the energy of each degree is "reflected" back to the comparable point on the other side of the rubber band. This becomes quite useful when you get a chart for some major event and it baffles you because you can't see any aspects. Toss in some solstice points for the planets and things can leap right out at you.

A solstice point is something like a "shadow" or "mirror" aspect, which gives you the secondary reading in the chart. It explains why you will find nitpicking Aries types and creative Libras, since their solstice points can fall in Virgo and Pisces.

When you are talking about your Moon's solstice points, you won't be surprised to learn that your personality readily picks up the attributes of the other sign which has the solstice point.

If you have a cluster of planets in one sign, you can easily see how it reflects back to its solstice point sign. Transits over a cluster of solstice points can sometimes be just as strong as transits over the actual positions of the planets. And you can understand why fixed sign people feel kicked in the teeth when heavy transits hit other fixed signs. It creates squares and oppositions to their natal positions AND to their solstice points.

The cardinals and mutables get the inconjuncts and sometimes semi-sextiles or sesquisquares—not quite as difficult.

Relocation Charts

I tried relocation charts for a while but have always ended up going back to the natal location for forecasting work. The only exception was when birth occurred in the other hemisphere. In that case, events "promised" by the natal don't always occur on time, and the life takes on the subtle pattern indicated in the relocation chart.

Other astrologers may have other opinions. I have never had a huge quantity of clients with births overseas (say in Europe or Asia) to give me a broad enough basis on which to judge with much confidence.

However, I am a firm believer in the Astro*Carto*Graphy methods pioneered so well by the late Jim Lewis. Those work and work well. Astro*Carto* Graphy is a technique whereby the position of one's natal planets is charted out on a world map, showing where each might be actually rising or on the MC. This is a technique which well repays a bit of study and should be in every astrologer's tool kit. Nowadays many computer astrology programs can give you a visual chart showing this.

For one thing, it allows you to help a client find a good place when considering relocation. Living on your Venus line is bound to be a happier choice than choosing a Saturn line for your next home.

The lines are surprisingly useful with mundane work. Looking at the charts of U.S presidents one can see where their "trouble spots" were in the world, for instance, during their terms of office. They often were where their Mars, Pluto or Saturn lines went.

As for some examples: John F. Kennedy's Pluto line ran through Dallas, where he was assassinated. Saturn was on his MC in Cuba, where the Bay of Pigs assault was a mortifying failure. Lyndon Johnson's Pluto line ran through Vietnam, and it was that war that killed his presidency. Richard Nixon had Uranus on the MC in China and it was the triumphant peak of his foreign policy to bring change to the US relations with the Chinese.

Oriental and Occidental

There is an imaginary line from the Sun in the chart to the opposite side of the zodiac, neatly dividing it in half. Whatever would be above the horizon if Sun were on the Ascendant is called oriental (eastern) or rising before the Sun comes up over the Ascendant. Anything that would be below it, following the Sun, is occidental (western) and is still in the sky when the Sun goes down.

Thus, if the natal Sun is in House 8, everything in Houses 2-7 is oriental. Well, whatever part of House 2 is less than 180 degrees from Sun, of course. Everything remaining is occidental.

This is why Venus is sometimes called a morning star and sometimes an evening star. Its proximity to Sun and its speed of travel means that sometimes it is in the sign before the Sun and other times is in the sign that follows the Sun. It's a common demonstration of how this works that we can see any time during the year if we pay attention.

There is also another use of these terms which has reference only to the natal chart and not to the Sun. This can prove quite confusing to a lot of people and is one reason the terms "oriental" and "occidental" are seldom used when talking about it. This is when oriental, or eastern, refers to the half of the chart on the entire left hand side, from MC to IC. The occidental then is the remaining half on the right side. It is a clear visual referral to the layout of the chart. The "oriental" side is thus comprised of houses 10, 11, 12, 1, 2 and 3. The remaining ones are "occidental," or western.

People with most of their planets in the oriental side of the chart are much more able to influence events in their lives. A good example comes in their careers. If unhappy in one spot, they take action and change jobs and can be quite good at picking a new one that offers better possibilities.

Those with occidental placements are not so lucky. If they find themselves unhappy in their jobs, no amount of action seems to make things happen until "the time is right." They are simply locked in to the present and must wait for an opportunity to unfold to which they may respond. It is quite as if the oriental side were dubbed "action" and the occidental side were dubbed "reaction."

Parans

You are sitting under a tree when Mercury is smack dab on Ascendant. You look at Mercury and off behind it you see a star. That's what's rising when Mercury does. Then you look overhead and see what star is on the MC when Mercury is rising. You have just found Mercury's two parans.

Later in the day when Mercury has moved past that position the parans are still the same. They are the stars which were rising and were on the MC when Mercury was on the Ascendant.

The Solar Return

For years I struggled in vain to use the solar return to my satisfaction. One of my students—a long-time student of another astrologer as well–however, was able to give me accurate information from a solar return that I didn't see how she got. Then she told me about Alexander Volguine, a French writer. I bought his book, *The Technique of Solar Returns,* as fast as I could haul out the money.

Volguine's premise is simple: each solar return house is read as if it falls into a natal house, partaking both of the natal influences and the solar return influences. **Sample:** The SR 2nd falls in the natal 7th. This shows that this year's income will depend heavily on partners, or strangers, or public relations, perhaps, but that in any case, the actions of others will strongly determine how much money you make (or spend).

Perhaps the natal 2nd house is ruled by Jupiter, but the solar return house is ruled by Saturn. Perhaps this year's (Saturn) spending obligations will be frustrated (or aided) by the generosity (Jupiter) or big-spending (Jupiter) of a partner or spouse.

The house into which the SR Ascendant and MC fall are key. So are the contacts of planets in the SR to the natal.

I don't want to try writing all the details of his book here but I hope that gives you a sample. I consider that book one of my half dozen most valuable texts. And I have a lot of books.

A Comet is Coming

What does an astrologer do with a comet? Comets come out of the darkness and jump into public consciousness for a brief while, swing around the Sun and disappear again. Only a few, such as Haley's Comet, have a reliable rotation in our solar system. It is thought that many simply escape our gravitational well and never return.

If you are a mundane astrologer you can say that if one comes out of late Capricorn, sign of government and those in public life, it may herald big changes in those things.

If you have charts with late Capricorn emphasized—such as at the time of a solar return—the comet definitely spells out change coming in the area of the SR chart where that degree of Capricorn falls.

Some of the older texts have a bit of material on what to expect from comets, depending on the area from which they come, or at least where they are first seen, but there is little written about them and what there is seems to be quite old. Or it doesn't seem to be very helpful. A lot of hot air and not much that is practical seems to collect around the topic. I have never found enough to suit me. It's frustrating because I think there is a lot more to say, and some comets obviously seem to herald very important world events. This is a fertile field for research and I would like to see someone do more with this topic.

A Library to Cherish

Books that we consider invaluable to our astrological development are not the same for everyone. Since I began studying in the 1950s, I learned from books that are now considered all but ancient. Many modern texts copy from them ruthlessly, however. At least one best seller I can think of grabbed whole gobs of material from Evangeline Adams, for instance. The author never bothered to cite her as the source, unfortunately.

It's always wise to use the originals if you can.

Here are a few books I treasure. The list is by no means complete and it's not in order of importance:

- *A to Z Delineator* by Llewelyn George
- *Heaven Knows What* by Grant Lewi
- Nicholas Devore's *Encyclopedia of Astrology*
- The two books by Evangeline Adams, *Your Place in the Sun* and *Your Place Among The Stars*
- *Nodes of the Moon* by E. Furze-Morrish
- *Simplified Horary Astrology* by Ivy Jacobson (add the rest of her volumes, too)
- *The Technique of Solar Returns* by Alexander Volguine
- *Electional Astrology* by Vivian Robson
- *Textbook of Modern Astrology* by Margaret Hone
- Set of *The American Ephemeris* volumes by Neil Michelsen
- A good table of houses and a table of proportional logarithms in case your computer breaks down and you (gasp!) actually have to calculate a chart by hand. *Dalton's Table of Houses* is still good.
- A bunch of current year ephemerides by the Rosicrucians that you can spread around the house near telephones and in your purse.
- *Degrees of the Zodiac* by E.C. Mathews (the only degree book I know in which the author did some actual research seeking similarities.)
- Nicholas Campion's *Book of World Horoscopes* and its companion book
- William Lilly's *Christian Astrology*

You'll notice these are not modern writers. It doesn't hurt to read the classics.

Chapter 11

Listening:
You don't have to predict

Some clients come to an astrologer just to talk.

I know that sounds odd, but it's true. They may or may not want you to throw in an astrological comment occasionally but they spend their entire consultation time talking about themselves or a problem they have. And then they leave without asking a thing about the future.

Should you still charge them your standard fee?

Of course.

Being a sounding board is a valid service. It's important for us to understand that we don't solve problems for people. People solve their own problems. Sometimes they like to get a forecast to see if their own thinking is on the right track, or they want to know if something is clouding their judgment.

Does that mean you should double up the time of their session so you can do your predicting? No. If they wanted it, they would have asked for it during the time they were allotted. And if they later decide they want to have it, they can come for another session.

But sometimes all they want is comfort, or hand holding and they want to tell their troubles to somebody who will care about them without judging them. Then, perhaps fortified by feeling they have found a friend, they will go off and solve their own problems.

This is OK. They paid you just for listening. Sometimes, to a troubled person, that's worth more than gold.

Chapter 12

When Your Client Arrives

Professional astrologers should be professional. No barefoot readings, please. If you are working for money, you should look like you deserve your fee. Skip the sweats and old tennies and for heaven's sake look at least as neat and proper as you would if you were asking the bank to loan you half a million dollars or so.

Once you're sure you pass muster, take a good look at your office, or the space where you meet your clients.. I mean, a **good look**. Walk in and stop and see what your eyes fall on first.

1. Is it clean? It should shine. No dusty tables, no dirty coffee mugs, and the floor should be immaculate. Keep the wastebasket emptied.

2. Is it neat? You may think it's cool to live in clutter. Go ahead. But don't expect your clients to think it's cool. If you are charging a decent price, clients have a right to expect tidy. Books should be on the shelves. Papers should be stacked aside neatly. Pencils and calculation stuff in drawers and only the files in front of you that you need. If in doubt, put it away.

3. Is it comfortable? Clients who are offered a chair that doesn't distract them from what you are saying are happier clients. A client in a soft, upholstered chair is getting a subliminal message that you are concerned for his or her well-being. If all you can afford is a folding chair, make sure it is a GOOD folding chair. Spend some of your first income for decent chairs.

4. Is the decor tasteful? For heaven's sake don't put up brown wallpaper with hunting scenes or pea green carpet if you want to run a good business. Color has a great bearing on how people feel and brown is depressing to some people. Pea green isn't so hot either. Get a book from the library on color if you are redecorating. Think soothing. Half the people who come to see astrologers are troubled. The other half wants to hear about themselves. Either way, you want them relaxed and upbeat.

5. What do you have on the table where you sit with your client? Some folks use a desk and that is OK if you like it, but a table can help you establish rapport more rapidly and is less intimidating for many clients. A small centerpiece is good. A bowl of flowers, perhaps, or a small bit of sculpture, or a pretty rock. It should not be large enough to be distracting, but it should be mildly interesting so that a client can look at it while you are hunting through the ephemeris for a good date for their vacation trip. A couple small curiosities—odd paper weights and the like, which can be handled by the nervous—are also good. A container with your business cards is a must. You want them to take a couple for their friends. If you have a printed brochure of your fees, have it handy.

6. Did you remember a box of tissues? Keep it close but out of sight. Some clients will start to weep readily (beware the Cancers) so you want to be able to whip out a tissue instantly if needed.

7. How's the light? Now take another look at your consulting area. Is there glare for your clients at certain times of the day? Rearrange the room to avoid that problem.

8. What about incense and scented candles? Personally, I'm not crazy about them for two reasons. First, they may irritate your clients. I know, I know, you're an expert at aromatherapy and you chose the apple cinnamon scent because it went with their moon/Mercury transit, but it can still annoy some people. Someone is bound to have asthma or hay fever or allergies and start sneezing. Secondly, they give the impression that you are somehow frivolous—a lightweight, with nothing of deep import to say. At the very least, you come across as weird, and who pays attention to weirdos anyway?

9. Do you provide recording for your clients? If not, do you make sure they have paper and pen or pencil to take notes? If your clients want to record, is there an electrical outlet available nearby for them to use? If not, get an extension cord and keep it available.

10. Do you add the thoughtful touches? Is there a convenient place for their coats or boots in winter? Do you offer to take their coats or help them on with them afterward? Did you remember to shake hands as they arrived and left? A little touching is a valuable thing. A gentle pat on the shoulder as you say goodbye can also convey encouragement.

All these questions should help you see your consulting space and how you use it with a fresh eye.

A few more things: Try not to use a timing device for your reading if at all possible. Put a clock on the shelf behind your clients where you can see it if you need to, but having something in front of them tick the time away is tacky.

Consider carefully any art objects in the room. You want nice but not wildly exciting. You are the star here, not your sculpture.

If you have done all this you will have given some serious thought to what makes people comfortable coming into your space. Clients may not seem to notice these things but they will go away with the impression that you cared about them.

And that's why you're an astrologer in the first place, isn't it?

Chapter 13

Who Are Your Clients?

Your clientele will be described by your 7th house. This is the house of the consultant—either the ones you hire or the one you become and it tells you who will want your services. If you have the Moon there or a planet in the 7th, aspecting your Moon, it can bring in lots of women and family packages.

Any aspect to Saturn will keep your repeat business large. Some of my clients I've been seeing for 30 years or more. Or I will see clients one year who haven't come for 12 years and 10 years later they pop in again.

Your pattern will be distinctive to you. Some get "the butcher, the baker, the candlestick maker." Some astrologers never see men at all, it seems. Others rarely see young people. If you have Mercury there, you may see a lot of young people.

I have Mars in House 7 and have done a lot of charts for doctors and nurses. Mars, of course, rules the medical profession and men generally. It's trine Jupiter, so I have also done tons of educators and teachers. My first client was a teacher. I also have Sun there and have done several people who owned their own businesses.

Many years ago I had a student with a poorly aspected 7th house and she told me she attracted really spooky clients. (I wouldn't open the door if I saw some of them in the driveway.) She was surprisingly comfortable about it when she had a man in the house, but when she was alone, it was a tad different. She told me she quit doing astrology for the public because she didn't like the people that came to see her. I didn't blame her.

Sometimes patterns change of course, and your progressions may bring you all women, for a while, or business clients, or all marriage counseling jobs etc. But the fundamental kind of people you serve are described by your 7th house.

All of us have certain areas of our charts where we are sensitive. We may have had the experience of finding that clients whose Sun or Moon signs are in those areas are difficult to interpret or perhaps to deal with on a personal level. Most of us in professional astrology learn to overcome that once we recognize what it is that annoys us or irks or angers us about a specific Sun sign.

Some of it is because we had a problem with someone like that previously, but I think it is also partly how each of our charts is arranged.

For some it may be the Mars contact. Other times it is a Saturn position.

I always find those with Scorpio Sun, Moon or Ascendant pretty direct and very easy to talk to as clients, despite the sign's reputation as secretive. Either they decide to level with you and you can talk turkey or they decide they won't tell you squat, but either way you know what you're dealing with.

Not so with some of the other signs. I have had clients that drove me up the wall because they were secretive about the wrong thing or wanted me to advise them about a situation they wouldn't actually open up and tell me about. Yes, you read that right. They wanted me to guess. Astrological patterns can include a wide range of situations. Picking just one and being sure it's the right one is not likely to happen. We don't have crystal balls, even though some people think we do.

One woman years ago spent way too much time talking to me. I couldn't get rid of her and I couldn't seem to help her. Every time I mentioned her chart showed she was having problems with her daughter she denied it. Finally it burst out (after about an hour and a half of denial). She wanted to give the child up for adoption because she feared she wasn't a good enough mother. It took another hour and a half to sort out as we talked her fears through. Then I never saw her again, so I don't know what happened or how the story ended. That's real life in the astrology office, of course. We are often frustrated by not knowing how it all comes out. I have a bunch of such unfinished tales still nagging me.

Anyway, her Sun fell on my Saturn. I know, I know--you all understand it was either karmic or it was going to be an important consultation. It was. I have never forgotten it for several reasons.

First of all, I needed to realize some people aren't going to talk until they have waltzed me around the mulberry bush for a while. I need patience. (That Saturn contact, of course.)

Second, just because people deny what I say I see doesn't mean I'm wrong. I need to trust myself.

Third, serious problems can walk in my door and I'd better do some praying ahead of time as well as afterwards lest I let both of us down. I need humility.

And those are just for openers.

Now I know that woman hadn't talked about her problem before. It took her too long to get to it. And she never came back, so she may have felt ashamed later that she did talk about it. It is important not to be judgmental when people tell you awful stuff and to convey that clearly. (Another lesson for me, of course).

And sometimes I have heard absolutely heart-breaking stories. We all do. But a wise man (much wiser than I) said something I try to remember. I forget it a lot, but I do try. He said, "Whenever anything disturbs me, no matter what it is or for whatever reason, something is the matter with me."

So whenever I get a client whose Sun sign is in the "wrong" spot, I suspect it will be an important reading for some reason or another. And if upsets me, I need to ask myself why.

Chapter 14

Predicting Death

Astrologers being seen as mere fortune tellers isn't acceptable to me. I also get very, very weary of the view that astrology is so much psycho babble instead of the useful tool we know it to be.

Frankly—and this is an opinion I have held for several years—I think the reason you get some astrologers saying "No no, let's not forecast" is because they can't do it and they have no confidence in their knowledge. Either they have let the scientific community grab their minds around the neck or they fear its opinions too much. In any case, they have spent more time on the hot air, than practicing their craft.

I just wonder why they're astrologers if they don't want to forecast. That's like becoming a meteorologist to discuss the shape of the clouds, but predict rain? Why, whatever do you mean?

I have heard the most incredible garbage from some supposedly good astrologers. It always tells me exactly where they are coming from. Somebody like Arch Crawford who comes right out and predicts market direction on TV has my respect. Sure, he isn't going to get it 100% right—nobody does. But he doesn't hide behind some advanced degree and then pretend prediction is beneath him. And I believe his newsletter record is No. 2 for accuracy among all stock market predictors. Some years it's been No. 1.

And as far as even a death prediction is concerned, I don't think that's automatically off limits, either, though it has become fashionable in recent years to consider it taboo. There are many times such information is of great value to a family member and if somebody wants to know—and is willing to pay the freight to find out—I think it should be available to them.

On the other hand, there's no sense in claiming we are infallible on such forecasting because we aren't and that is not a forecast I would ever make lightly for anyone. But I have had clients with seriously ill elderly parents, for instance, who needed a time frame. One long-time client was deeply grateful to me for helping prepare her for her father's death after an illness lasting many years. She was able to approach it much more calmly and help her mother when the difficult time arrived.

Another client was dealing with her husband who was bedridden with Alzheimer's. The case was hopeless (as they all are) and had lasted for many years. She was desperate to know when there would be some relief for her from the long burden of care-giving. Should I not have helped her?

It's easy to say we shouldn't do this or we shouldn't do that. But I think such opinions need to be tested by doing business as an astrologer and using some common sense tempered with some compassion for the people who need answers.

When the chips are down people want straightforward, reasonable accuracy. Then do your best and be at peace about it, even if you are wrong. Don't pretend you are infallible, and help your clients understand this.

The limit of anyone's responsibility to help others is "opportunity" and "ability." You use your ability to the best you can when you have the opportunity. You have neither the right nor ability to tell someone involved in his/her life what to do. You can suggest ideas when you have the opportunity of a reading. But when the client goes out the door, your role has ended. So has your "responsibility."

One must simply let go and let God—or the Universe—manage the situation. The most any one of us can do after that may be to pray for our clients. Sometimes that means praying for more than one person--one who is injuring others through selfishness and one who may be injured, for instance. This is the same principle to apply on giving death information. Pray for the one who is dying and the one who is trying to help them with their last steps.

And be sure to study techniques that will give you better answers. You may not cook a turkey more than once in a year but you need to know HOW. It goes with the job.

Chapter 15

Planetary Amulets

A friend once asked me what I thought about the idea that a planetary amulet could "correct" the effect of a bad aspect.

The whole idea of wearing an amulet linked to a planetary energy is to help attune one to a favorable influence. The idea is that it thus mitigates harmful influences that bring problems into our lives.

This is an idea that comes out of medieval astrology and there are people who still believe it works and use it. Those who want help with love or money may seek a Venus amulet, for instance, to help align themselves with those energies. There are astrologers who will provide an amulet for a fee or even help you create your own.

It's not an area I ever explored, frankly, but I have a few comments that may be useful to those who want to do so.

First, it's very important to understand your own chart before choosing an amulet. And it is even more important to understand the influence each planet has.

Consider for a moment what happens astrologically when transiting or progressed Mars or Saturn aspects a chart which has a natal square between those two planets. It does not bring good things, as any experienced astrologer can tell you. It intensifies the energy that is already there. A natal square between the two malefics is seldom a good thing.

So, if you were born when Mars and Saturn were promising trouble in your life, the last thing I should think you would want to do is to bring more of it by using a Mars or Saturn amulet, even if one was promised to "improve" the way Mars or Saturn works in your life.

The natal chart is the root from which the tree grows. You cannot change the root, only help it grow or hinder its manifestation.

You may think that a solar return with a trine between two natally afflicted planets can bring about better conditions for the individual. This is temporarily true, as far as it goes. But it will still act within the parameters of the natal chart. We grow only slowly and within the rules of our own being.

A solar return is a transit, a passing influence out of one's control, and not at all the same thing as a deliberate attempt to avoid difficulties in the natal pattern by wearing a talisman which intensifies those energies.

If--and I say if--you have an unafflicted placement which you wish to use more efficiently, then perhaps a combination would work. A natal Mars trine Jupiter, perhaps, could be boosted for someone, having these energies linked in a positive way or even almost linked.

However, I think simple logic would forbid putting together two such inimical forces as Mars and Saturn, planets of hot and cold. Mars and Jupiter relate to each other--Mars and Saturn do not.

Anyone with a bad aspect between two planets should never wear a talisman that intensifies the energy of either one, in my opinion. I think it especially applies to Mars and Saturn since they are already at opposite ends of the spectrum. However, you would not want a Sun/Mars amulet if you have a natal square between those two, either. A natal trine would be favorable, of course. But if you have it, you're already a bundle of drive and energy so why would you want to intensify it?

Someone with a natal sextile between Moon and Jupiter might thus benefit from linking those energies in a silver and turquoise piece. Silver is the metal of the moon and the turquoise is a Jupiter stone. We see people adopt unconscious mitigation of harmful energies all the time. Leos wear gold, Capricorns like black, etc.

In the late Barbara Cameron's books on Burmese astrology she includes a great deal of information on mitigation techniques used in that ancient system. She specifically warns against attempting to intensify what is not good in a natal pattern.

It is a valid principle which clearly seems to apply to amulets as well.

It seems only common sense to me.

Chapter 16

Helping Your Children

Astrologers who are parents have a double burden. You want the best for your children and you may think you know exactly what that is. And you may put too much pressure on them and that's not fair. They aren't your clients.

If you are asked for advice or help, give it. Otherwise, shut up. Advise, but don't insist. We shouldn't try to take over our children's lives. It isn't good for them and it isn't good for us. You can't manage your children into getting good aspects for everything. Choosing a date to do something is a good example

If your daughter is determined to have a big fancy Saturday night wedding on a day with rotten aspects and she hasn't asked your opinion on it, then she'll do it and the fact that she picks a lousy date or time will be part of her own destiny. It's her life. I know that's tough to accept sometimes when it's your child, but it's the only way to go. Otherwise you risk driving her away and she'll do what she wants to do then anyway.

Marriage charts are funny. Over the years I have learned that truly compatible couples with happy prospects select good dates all by themselves without the aid of astrologers. When couples don't choose good dates, there is usually a reason why—their charts aren't compatible or they have some special lessons to learn. Sometimes the marriage won't even happen for any one of a number of reasons.

If it's your child and you see a problem, of course, you want to fix it. But when people select a void-of-course Moon, for instance, and resist your counsel on it, my best advice is to stay out of it. If the thing goes sour, you don't want to be blamed. If it goes well, the couple will take the credit themselves.

This is quite different if they **ask** for your help. Then you are free to wade right in and give it your best shot.

But when they don't seem pleased with your help, act stubborn when you offer or "forget" your helpful hints, then just stay out. They have a road to take and you can't convince them to use another route.

We all want our children to be happy. But what if you fix something you shouldn't to make it more stable only to realize 20 years down the pike that they should never have stayed together and they would have parted long ago if you had left the situation alone in the first place?

As astrologers we do not, most emphatically not, run the universe. We will all be called to account one day for what we have said and done and I don't want the karma I would get if I tried to micro-manage my kids and made their lives worse in the process. Besides, your relationship with your children is far more important than anything else. Keep that in mind. It helps when you see them heading for a bad date.

Chapter 17

Condense Your Readings

If you are spending too long on a chart and trying to include every detail of the client's life, you will waste both your time and your client's and will find yourself working unrealistically long hours. You need to learn to condense your session.

The first thing you need to do is practice writing a single sentence which describes this person, and includes a bit of the Sun, Moon and Ascendant. It has to be something you can say in one breath, too. No thousand-word jumbos allowed. If you find this hard to do, you need additional practice.

Here are some exercises on how to read a chart:

1) Time yourself. You have one hour flat. Divide the chart into three areas: Love, Money and Health. You get 15 minutes each to talk about the subjects from the natal point of view and the current outlook for the year ahead. The last 15 minutes is for questions. Don't gasp. It gets worse.

2) Write down a few key words to help you tell the person about each area. Your client does not want to know about the meaning of their Sun or Moon. They do want to know about their marriage or their love affair or their kids, how their job is going and when or if they will get a raise and about their health or lack of it.

3) Practice with a recorder talking about one of the three areas I mentioned. When you can do one area in 15 minutes, start another. Remember, that when it comes to really reading the chart to a person, your enthusiasm will probably run away with you, but if you have a "15-minute clock" in your head, you won't do much more than 20 minutes without shifting topics.

4) Recognize that what I am giving you is like a chastity belt: It won't stop you from getting into trouble, but it will make you uncomfortable enough to do something about it before you wreck the project.

I have suggested an unduly restrictive regimen for a reason. Yes, you can spend more time if you wish. Yes, you can tell people about their Sun or Moon if they wish, but you need the discipline of practicing within a tight time limit to force your brain to synthesize.

Back in my days as an editor, I often had to tell reporters to sum up their story in a lead sentence, so that people knew what they were about to read. This is tough for beginners and a lot of reporters are Virgos, surprisingly enough. Summing up is often tough for Virgos. Learning this technique made them better writers. That sentence I suggest you write before you "do" a chart is an astrological lead sentence.

Always hunt for the positive alternative if you see roadblocks in your readings. I should probably say that twice.

Sometimes you may see the focus will be on career for the next couple years. If you tell someone, "Yes, a new relationship would be nice and comforting" but you know from their chart that their focus is going to be in the career area for a while, they will accept putting love on the back burner for now. Most people know that they can't give their "all" to more than one thing at a time.

Or, you may tell someone that right now the only kind of person you can see that they would attract would be a real loser, and that the universe seems to be protecting them from that, it is comforting, rather than the reverse.

Sometimes people are coming out of a bad marriage and they think they want somebody to replace the "partner" role in their lives immediately. When you help them understand that this is a rebuilding time for their inner strength and a time to prepare for the better aspects down the road, they understand. Nobody wants to meet a possible second mate when the aspects that just ended their rotten marriage will only bring in another loser. It takes time for the wheel to turn, right?

If they ask about a bad health problem, they already are worried, or they already fear they won't get better. If that's what you see, refer them to competent medical sources but don't lie. You can agree, "Yes, I can see this is a very serious medical problem and will need a lot of treatment." and you can admit you haven't all the answers about their health.

It is not a sin for an astrologer to say, "I don't know." Besides, if I fear the worst, I fall back on my absolutely last resource. I tell them:

a) I am not medically trained

b) I am not God and can be dead wrong about what I see, and

c) I don't want to mislead with either false hope or excessive pessimism. And then I shut up.

If I see good aspects coming, I may tell them treatments improve things at that time. If I see bad aspects, I may say there will be difficulties then. I try not to mislead.

Hopefully you won't run into problems that you can't assist with in some way. Some of those come from people who are usually trying to help others.

There are two signs of the Zodiac that are always on a mission to fix the rest of us: Virgo and Aquarius. Virgo wants to fix us one by one and Aquarius wants to fix us in bunches (using politics or social change or e-mail newsletters or whatever).

It always amuses me when people stand up and holler like their signs. But then, I must be getting old, because more things amuse me than ever. I can hardly get through a day without a good belly laugh, or a guffaw, and sometimes a knee slapper that I hadn't planned on.

Today I had a Capricorn client who, as I was closing her reading said, "Now, Pat, I want to know all the rest of the bad stuff you haven't told me." I almost slid under the table laughing. She's a longtime client and student, so she appreciated the joke after she realized what she said. Talk about pessimistic! Only Capricorns ever seem to come up with that one. No wonder so many Capricorns become comedians. It's in the genes.

Chapter 18

Giving Bad News

Telling a client something unpalatable is a really hard thing for astrologers to do sometimes. But I always remember what a tough city editor taught me when I was a reporter: You can say absolutely anything in print if you know how to say it. You can also tell a client absolutely anything. The key is knowing HOW to say it. A few things help.

1) Always-- but always --pray before you read a chart. I believe God uses us to help people and if you are willing to put your own ego aside and genuinely try to help your client, the words you need are ones you will find.

2) Consider the chart you have. A **watery type** needs sympathy and very gentle handling. Keep the tissues handy. **Earthy people** want you to offer some practical answers to their problems. Have a couple in mind before they get there. **Air types** can be detached apparently but they will want to talk about it all… a lot. Double the time you allotted for their reading if they're having serious problems. **Fire people** may go all dramatic on you (watch out for the Leo moon here) but most prefer straight talk.

    Scorpios want you to just say it, Aquarians want you to pretend it's about a friend (not them, heavens no) and they'll take you all the way to Pittsburgh and back before they level with you. Each sign has its own way of dealing with things.

3) Always remember you can be wrong. But if you really believe something needs saying, say it as tactfully and plainly as you can. Act like it's no big deal to you. As I tell clients, we all have problems, they're just in different areas.

4) Unless the client wants to talk about their sex life, don't hit them over the head with it. I learned this the hard way with a very skittish woman some years ago. We were talking about her lover and I accidentally referred to the lover as "she." This poor dear was so deep into the closet she was in *Narnia* and I later learned from a relative that she was terribly upset I knew and that she would never come back to me out of embarrassment.

If people want to talk about something, a few gentle questions may help them, but if there is resistance, let it be. This is their reading, not yours. If you start to talk about something you think needs saying and they turn you off, don't belabor the point. Sometimes all you need is to plant a seed and they'll do the rest of the work on their own.

5) Don't take it too hard if you screw up. Chalk it up to being human and go on.

6) Some clients don't want the truth. They want pipe dreams. I never feed the pipe dreams. I had a client (still have) who came to me 30 years ago all ga ga over some married man and I told her bluntly, over and over, that she didn't have a prayer with him. She cried--a lot. Years later she told me she still gets annoyed when I won't tell her what she wants to hear but she knows she can always count on me for the truth. (Boy was that a long time coming.) Whenever she needs the truth she calls me up.

7) Keep praying for your clients after they're gone. What's that old saw? "More things have been wrought by prayer than this world dreams of." We all need prayers.

The most important thing to remember is that a client never wants to hear about the astrologer. The client wants to hear about 'me.'

Don't talk about yourself. Talk about your client. Don't say, "I think you should." Say, "these aspects suggest you could use energy to do thus and so," or "this pattern shows why you have difficulty with budgeting."

Your experiences have made you who you are. OK, fine. The client wants to know what the chart can say about his or her experiences.

A good gimmick is to have a piece of paper handy and practice a reading. Mark an X for every time you say the word "I" and an "O" for every time you say "you." We say "I" so many times without thinking that when you try to watch yourself you'll be surprised.

Make it a rule not to discuss personal experiences or personal opinions, if at all possible. The truth is people don't care and it's their nickel.

There is an exception. There is one sun sign that does want to know about the astrologer. Every time I have ever read for a Libra, the first thing they say after we are done is,

"Tell me about yourself...how did you get into this," or some other question. It is an absolutely charming trait.

Chapter 19

Dangerous Computers

I think the scenario of too much computerized astrology haunts a lot of us who look down the road at some aspects ahead. What would we do if the world took a "bad turn," and civilization stepped backward or there was major interference with electronic devices? All too many astrologers would see the instant end of their astrology career.

Why? Because they rely too much on the machine and not enough on themselves.

I'm not sure if my concern is because I am picking up (psychically, perhaps) on alternate futures or are simply trying to cover the possibilities. But JIC--Just In Case--it doesn't hurt to learn to make soap. It's always a good, amusing hobby.

Some of my JIC favorites: spinning yarn off the beast (any beast with fur will do), knitting or weaving it into clothing, socks, mittens, hats, misc., stockpiling books on herbal remedies, edible wild plants and how to make yurts, the best way to make compost, etc. etc.

Keep a fireplace that works with wood. I've used mine to fix dinner several times when the power went out during storms.

Oh, yes, and it also doesn't hurt to keep books on hand calculation of charts handy, along with algorithm sheets, tables of houses, etc., if you plan to do astrology when there's no power for your lap top.

One good magnetic storm could wipe your computer of everything you know, even if you and civilization survived. It pays to carry the information in your own head. There is plenty of evidence that magnetic storms from the sun have caused severe damage at various times in the earth's history. They could happen again. And of course, a nearby nuclear blast could do it, too. That's a scenario we don't even want to think about, of course.

But relying on canned interpretations? Jeeeeeez, no. If the canned stuff goes, so does your astrology.

If you didn't learn to cast a chart by hand when you got into astrology, get a good text and teach yourself how. Better yet, find a teacher. It will do a great deal for your self-confidence, to say nothing of giving you a better comprehension of how the solar system works. And that's bound to improve your work. Oh, and you have to do that anyway if you want to pass a competency test. So go for it.

Just last week a woman called to ask me if I'd teach her calculation for her test and I told her, "No." First of all, I haven't actually hand-calculated one in probably 30 years myself and second because I didn't want to make a mistake teaching her house cusp correction. She needs somebody who's been doing it more recently.

All of which proves my point. I'm too lazy to actually go to the files and dig out the material and start hand calculating again when I have a perfectly wonderful computer program. But if I actually had to do it, it wouldn't take me long to brush up. Once you've spent a few years doing something it stays in your brain. Sure, the storage closet where you keep the information is probably dusty and has some cobwebs, but it's there.

And that's the important thing.

Chapter 20

The Matter of Referrals

Astrologers are not physicians. We can analyze the health pattern of an individual, and tell if you are currently a little sick, pretty sick or desperately ill, and even perhaps where the problem areas might be found. But true medical help, diagnosis and treatment belongs in a doctor's office.

People who have a fear of doctors, for whatever reason, sometimes want help from alternate sources first. And yes, we can tell if you have allergies, or lactose intolerance or migraine tendencies. But let me tell you a story about a client of mine.

She came with a friend and had said she just wanted a general reading. But I nearly had a stroke when I was preparing her work because of the life-threatening aspects I saw. I flat out told her I didn't want to waste her time and mine with "stuff" when what she really needed was to go see a doctor immediately.

She was, to say the least, startled when I wouldn't read for her. I wouldn't take her money and I spent her entire visit insisting that she not look to me for her answers but go see a doctor. Before the two women left, the friend told me she thought the woman was ill and had been trying in vain to get her to ask for medical help. My urging finally got her off the dime.

Some weeks later I learned she had been desperately ill, as I surmised, and her doctor was able to operate on a large, malefic tumor and get her blood sugar under control (diabetes, too) and she got well. She called me months later to say thanks for saving her life.

Astrologers have limitations. Yes, we can do some things. But if you think you have a serious medical problem, see a doctor. If you think your client does, send her or him to a doctor. It's good astrology.

Chapter 21

When Your Clients Leave

When your clients leave, do they take anything with them except a happy memory? If not, you may have missed a golden opportunity to build your business. And let's face it, all other things aside, if you are doing astrology for money, it's a business. And if you want to keep on doing it, you need to eat and pay the rent so repeat business is important.

What should your clients take? For one thing, every client should walk out the door with your business card in purse or pocket. Those little cards have a way of resurfacing when the client needs counseling or is in a difficult time period and will come back to see you.

Not every client will go to the extreme that one of mine did. Fifteen years after our first session he wanted to talk to me again. He couldn't find my card, he forgot my last name and he didn't remember the name of my street. But he got in his car and drove persistently up and down area highways until something looked familiar and he found my street. He wasn't sure of my house (I'd changed the color) but he hopped out and banged on my door and when I answered he grinned from ear to ear.

We made an appointment and after his session he took a handful of business cards which he said he would stash in various places so 15 years from now if he wants to see me again, he'll be able to find me.

Make yourself easy to find. Give a business card to your clients every time. In fact, clip it to a copy of the chart.

Now most people can't read the chart. They know that, of course. But the chart blank should have your name, address and phone number on it, and they paid for the chart so they should have a copy of it. People like to have their charts.

You don't have to make a production out of it in a fancy folder with an analysis unless you charge a fancy price for the reading and can justify the extra effort. Most folks just look at a paper chart, fold it up and stash in a pocket or purse. But they take it.

If you have a program that gives them information about it, and you feel it is a nice touch you want to add, go ahead. I don't do it, but if you want to, go for it.

Many clients ask if they can tape their reading. By all means say yes. They will take away a record of their session that is a concrete reminder of what you have said. Few people have an eidetic memory. They just plain forget half of what you tell them. A tape is a way they can review the message.

And sometimes the tape alone will bring them back. Many replay it at the end of the year's forecast and I have had clients tell me they were stunned to realize I had pinpointed all the major action of the time period. It's a kind of verification that is priceless, both to them and to you.

Best of all, if you find you missed a lot of stuff, it is an indication that the chart is not correct. Or, they will tell you that you were off consistently on all forecasts by a month. That kind of feedback is invaluable in making the new predictions.

If your client does not have a tape recorder, be sure to provide paper and pen or pencil so they can take notes. Make sure they remember to take the notes. Again, it provides a concrete reminder for them to use and allows you to get feedback on the forecasting.

A word on feedback. If you don't think you need it, you are wrong. We all need to know how we're doing. Feedback from the client tells us where we are right, where we are wrong, and where we need improvement. More than that, it shows us how This Particular Chart operates. Each chart is different—and a few years' feedback helps you do a better job for a client. It is the doorway to improvement of our skills.

So what else could a client take when they leave?

If you have a brochure printed with your fees and a list of the services you can provide, be sure to give one to each client.

Some astrologers have fancy computer analyses and prediction programs and like to have a long printout for a client. I don't do this for this reason: I find they can confuse clients sometimes. I had a client call me once when I first began doing this and ask why the canned analysis was different than mine and which was the right one.

With all due respect to those who write these programs and provide the analyses, if we aren't talking the same language, it's no help to anybody. I stopped using one.

Is there anything else a client should take? I think every client should get a warm sendoff. A hand shake, a wish that he or she will have a good year, perhaps a pat on the shoulder and words of encouragement if the client is going through tough times. These are real people who are trusting us with a piece of their lives. Handle with care.

But for heaven's sake, if you don't do anything else, **make sure they take your business card.**

Chapter 22

The Apple Tree

You have to have both feet on the ground if you want to be of help to your fellow human beings.

Being an astrologer is not exactly the same thing as running over with a casserole when the neighbor is ill. It is more like holding up a mirror to help someone figure out if they are who they want to be and if they are going where they want to go. Until you have asked yourself the same questions, you may not be ready to do this.

If you begin to study your own psyche, it is amazing how much you learn about those of other people. The self is like a locked room full of furniture and stored possessions, cluttered, and dusty. It contains our experiences, memories, opinions, emotions, hopes, fears, joys and plans for the future. We seldom even ask ourselves what's in there.

Going in and turning on the light and looking around is quite a revelation. The process takes time and determination. Most of us think of the self as a storeroom for treasure, full of good things that we can be proud of. We seem highly reluctant to examine it too closely, however. This is because we really don't want to disturb our good opinion of our selves.

When we actually look, we may be appalled to discover that it contains things like bad temper, greed, selfishness and much worse. We find that we are not the wonderful people we thought we were. It's surprising how often that comes as a shock. It's a very humbling experience and frankly, quite good for us.

In fact, the seven deadly sins are no stranger to any of us. We all contain within ourselves the seeds of all the bad—or all the good—possibilities in the world. It is up to us to choose which seeds to 'water.'

Until we have taken some conscious steps to try to nurture the good seeds and have begun to make an effort to weed out the bad ones and clean out the dust and debris we have found, we aren't ready to help others. But once we have begun this work, it is surprising how much insight it lends us. We suddenly see that we are just like everybody else—no better, no worse, but merely human.

What you recognize within yourself, you see just as readily in others, and knowing how tender your own feelings are, you can begin to handle those of others gently, too.
But that's only the first step. Learning about one's self is a lifelong task, and we should be realistic about it. Perfection is not around the corner. You have to be able to forgive yourself for not getting there overnight. Once you realize you aren't as good as you want yourself to be, you will stop expecting others to be as good as you want them to be.

Somebody wiser than I said, "The proper study of mankind is man." I'd say it a little more personally: "The proper study of a human being is the self." Women have to do the work just as well as men, so there's no weaseling out over terminology.

The next step is to learn how to give yourself truly good care. That's how you learn to care for others. You have to provide for yourself what you know you need, even if you aren't in the mood to do it. Then when you suggest that somebody else do something good for themselves, you know what you're saying.

Back in the dark ages when I smoked like a chimney, I knew perfectly well that I should tell the puffing Gemini I was counseling not to smoke because he needed fresh air for good health. But it was a hard sell, let me tell you. What, you think I should have told him, "Don't do what I do, do what I say"?

Right.

You have to deal with a lot of problems if you want to be an astrologer. It helps to have survived your own intact. Your clients don't want to hear yours of course, they have their own. But you can't avoid dealing with your own by spending all your time on theirs, either. It doesn't work and it just wastes your time.

A wise man in the Bible said you first have to take the 2 x 4 out of your own eye before you worry about the splinter in your neighbor's eye.

If you want to survive someone else's problems, you also have to let them go when you are done learning about them. When the client goes out the door, so should the problem. Detachment is the key to keeping your own sanity.

Does this mean you shouldn't remember their difficulty, or be ready to aid or counsel if asked? No, but it does mean that when the distressed person leaves, so should their distressful emotions. If you involve yourself emotionally in their problems you don't help anyone and you don't help yourself either. Remember, you are advisor, not the manager of anyone's life except your own.

Get in the habit of having an outlet after a reading. Maybe it's mowing the lawn, or playing with the kids, or going for a long walk. But have some physical activity waiting for the end of a reading and you will find it easier to let go of a client's problems and the accompanying stress.

You can't be a help to anybody if you are overworked. Don't do so many readings that you can't handle the stress. Cut back. If you aren't making enough money, get another job and do fewer charts. But do the ones you do well.

Don't take it too much to heart if you haven't helped someone solve all their problems. You never will. Most of the time we just plant ideas and it's up to the client to decide what to do about them. It helps to remember that's what this whole free will notion is about.

We advise and counsel, but they decide on the outcome and that's the way it's supposed to work.

Your real job is your own growth. Every person is responsible for that. You can't convince a client to be something he isn't ready to be anymore than you can force feed a tomato plant and turn it into a cherry tree.

Opportunity and ability are the measure of responsibility. Once you have gone as far as opportunity and ability can take you, let it go. Your job is done. It's up to the universe to take it from there.

If you want to be of service to your fellow man, I will tell you a secret. You must be like an apple tree by the road, dispensing your apples to all who pass by. It doesn't matter if they "deserve" the apples or whether they will use them wisely for good pies or not—that's not your job to judge, anyway. Your job is just to make the apples and give them away. The rest is out of your hands.

Be an apple tree astrologer and I guarantee you that you will help your fellow human beings.

About the Author

Pat Geisler

Pat Geisler began her professional practice of astrology in 1969 and has written, lectured and taught for many years in northern Ohio, nationally and internationally. She retired from her consulting work in 2011.

Also newly published in 2013, is Pat's much longer and very comprehensive book, entitled, ***The Plain Vanilla Astrologer***. In this book she teaches a wide variety of techniques that she has found useful over her long, successful career as a consulting astrologer. Charts are included to demonstrate many of the techniques, and you'll also read and learn from Pat's experiences in consulting.

Pat is a member of AFAN, ISAR and NCGR, and her writings have appeared in their publications as well as on several websites.

She is also a retired journalist with state and national awards.

Pat is a widow with four children and five (superior) grandchildren. Her home is in Grafton, Ohio.

The title of this new book by

Pat Geisler

comes from a nickname given her by her students and friends. It speaks to her no nonsense approach based on many years of experience as a counseling astrologer and as an astrology teacher—using whatever methods would best inform and assist her clients and students.

In *The Plain Vanilla Astrologer* you'll read about a wide variety of astrological techniques in common use by most astrologers, but you'll also learn about several older methods found in very few, if any, current books. You'll view 33 charts as Pat tells you about them. Her style is informal, while still very informative, and sometimes sparks a chuckle—such that the reader can easily imagine how it must have been to be a student in a class Pat was teaching—and enjoying it very much, while also gaining a wealth of useful information.

This is not a first book for beginners. It assumes that the reader knows the basics of astrology. It's not a formal textbook, either. It covers a wealth of astrological techniques in a way that illuminates them. It's far more about how Pat sees things, and it made this reader wish I lived closer to where she is so I could get together with her often, just to chat for awhile.
—Maria Kay Simms

The Plain Vanilla Astrologer
48 Chapters, 33 Charts
366 pages
$19.95

ACS Publications, an imprint of Starcrafts LLC
Epping, New Hampshire, (603) 734-4300
www.astrocom.com

With *The Electronic Astrologer*

You can learn more about astrology, and do charts and reports on your home computer ... it's easy, even for the newest beginner, yet still has the power to please experienced astrologers!

For Windows XP, Vista or 7. Works well on Mac with PC emulator.

With **Reveals Your Horoscope,** you can easily calculate a natal chart for anyone for whom you have birth data.

With **Reveals Your Future**, you have a comprehensive guide to your future based on secondary progressions, transits, eclipses and lunations.

With **Reveals Your Romance**, you can analyze and rate the romantic compatibility of any two individuals. The special score sheet is fun—and revealing—to use!

Print charts & very extensive reports!

Each program — $74.95
Or, buy "all three"—
the *Series* package—for **$175.**

Programmed by Rique Pottenger
Interpreted text by Maritha Pottenger, Zipporah Dobyns and Maria Kay Simms.

includes built in ACS Atlas
See sample reports on our website!

www.astrocom.com
866-953-8458

The American Ephemeris Series

Standard setting reference works by Neil F. Michelsen and Rique Pottenger, now available in new editions!

BMBT $19.95

BNAE21M $26.95

BNAE20M $29.95

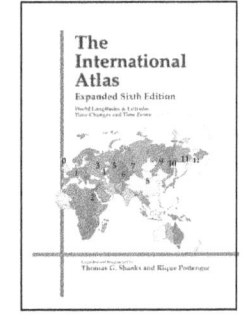
B1A6E $39.95

BASE2001 $32.95

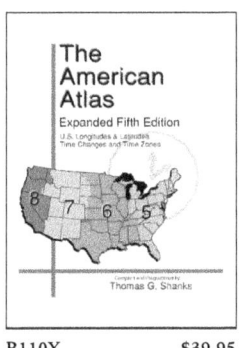
B110X $39.95

BAHE21 $34.95

BDEC0720 $19.95

B106X $19.95

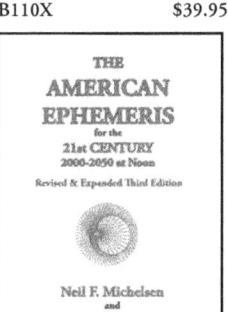
BASE21N $19.95

BNME0620 $21.95

AE5050N $29.95

BASTE2 $26.95

BTPP3 $32.95

BNAE20N $29.95

B223X $24.95

prices subject to change without notice

Personalized Astrology Lessons

The only correspondence course that teaches you astrology with examples from your personal horoscope.

P.A.L.S

PAL LESSON TOPICS

1. Introducing Astrology: Planets, Signs and Houses 2.The Glyphs and More on Planets & Signs 3. The Astrological Alphabet 4. More on Planets in Signs 5. More on Planets in Houses 6. Elements and Qualities 7. Rulers—Natural & Actual 8. Introducing Aspects 9. Learning to Spot Aspects & Meanings 10. Interpreting Planetary Aspects 11. Integrating Houses & Signs with Planetary Aspects 12. More on Synthesizing 13. More Themes 14. Spotting Repeated Themes 15. Odds Ends (retrogrades, stations, house systems, interceptions & more) 16. Odds & Ends Continued (exaltaton, fall, detriment, rulers & more) 17. Odds & Ends Continued (East Point, Vertex, Moon's Nodes & more) 18. Identifying Life Areas in the Horoscope 19. Analyzing Basic Identity 20. Analyzing Career 21. Analyzing Relationships 22. Analyzing Mind & Communication 23.Analyzing Parents 24.Mother & Father 25. Analyzing Children & Creativity 26. Analyzing Financial Prospects 27. Analyzing Beliefs & Values 28l Analyzing Sensuality & Sexuality 29. Kar

These lessons offer you an opportunity to master the age-old discipline of astrology, and will empower you to look deeper into all the issues of your life. Enhance your self-esteem and discover your highest potential. Maritha Pottenger created these lessons to help those curious beginners to understand all the tools that astrology has to offer. With an activist approach to astrology, Maritha shows you how to create your future and the life you want! Reinforce these lessons with actual homework assignments that test your knowledge! Please specify Lesson Numbers when ordering.

All 32 Lessons on 1 chart with Notebook
PAL ALL-BOW1..$99.95
One Lesson PAL-BOW1......................................5.95

Any 6 Lessons on 1 chart PAL6-BOW1......$24.95
Notebook only NB-BOW1..................................8.95

Prices subject to change. Shipping & handling will be added.

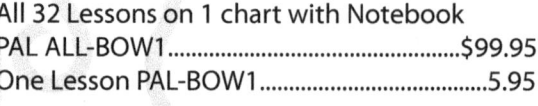

ASTRO COMPUTING SERVICES
Starcrafts LLC, PO Box 446, Exeter, NH 03833

www.astrocom.com

Come visit Astro Computing Services at www.astrocom.com !

Since founded by Neil F. Michelsen in 1973, Astro has served astrologers worldwide at all levels: beginner, intermediate, professional!

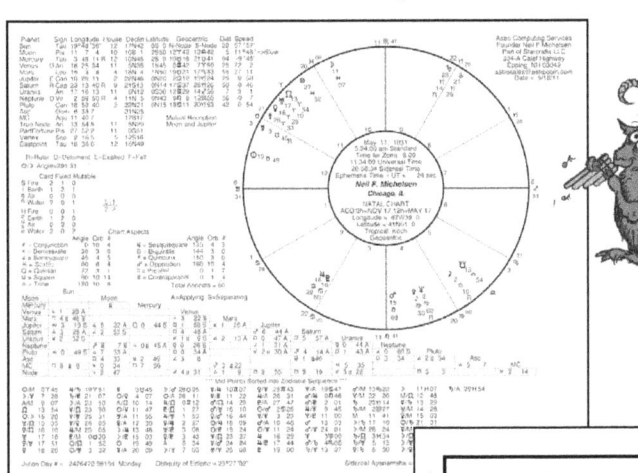

This is still our most popular chart—with more info on one page than any other, & with endless options!

We have lots of other chart styles too, from very complex to clean & easy. Here are two samples of our matted Art Charts, available in five different Astro'toon sets. That's our company chart on the right, with the Ram...

You'll find lots of books to help you learn, a wide variety of interpreted reports . . .

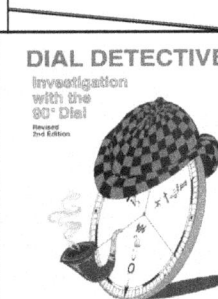

and software, too!

C'mon, now...

Log on & see what we've got for you!

astrocom.com

www.ingramcontent.com/pod-product-compliance
Lightning Source LLC
Chambersburg PA
CBHW081501040426
42446CB00016B/3349